T0373588

RussiaGate and Propaganda

This book furthers our understanding of the practice of propaganda with a specific focus on the RussiaGate case.

RussiaGate is a discourse about alleged Russian "meddling" in US elections, and this book argues that it functions as disinformation or distraction. The book provides a framework for a better understanding of ongoing developments of RussiaGate, linking these to macroconsiderations that rarely enter mainstream accounts. It demonstrates the considerable weaknesses of many of the charges that have been made against Russia by US investigators, and argues that this discourse fails to take account of broader non-transparent persuasion campaigns operating in the election-information environment that are strengthened by social media manipulation. RussiaGate has obscured many of the factors that challenge the integrity of democratic process in the USA. These deserve a much higher priority than any influence that Russia may want to exert. The book concludes that RussiaGate discourse needs to be contextualized with reference to a long-established broader competition between great powers for domination of EurAsia. This pitches the USA/European Union against Russia/China and perhaps, ultimately, even the USA against Europe.

This book will be of much interest to students of media and communication studies, propaganda studies, US politics, Russian politics, and International Relations in general.

Oliver Boyd-Barrett is Professor Emeritus at Bowling Green State University and California State Polytechnic University, USA.

RussiaGate and Propaganda

Disinformation in the Age
of Social Media

Oliver Boyd-Barrett

Routledge
Taylor & Francis Group

LONDON AND NEW YORK

First published 2020
by Routledge
2 Park Square, Milton Park, Abingdon, Oxon OX14 4RN

and by Routledge
52 Vanderbilt Avenue, New York, NY 10017

Routledge is an imprint of the Taylor & Francis Group, an informa business

British Library Cataloguing-in-Publication Data
A catalogue record for this book is available from the British Library

Library of Congress Cataloging-in-Publication Data
Names: Boyd-Barrett, Oliver, author.
Title: RussiaGate and propaganda : disinformation in the age of
    social media / Oliver Boyd-Barrett.
Description: Abingdon, Oxon ; New York, NY : Routledge, 2020. |
    Includes bibliographical references and index.
Identifiers: LCCN 2019016498 | ISBN 9780367202620 (hardback) |
    ISBN 9780429260537 (e-book)
Subjects: LCSH: Presidents—United States—Election—2016. |
    Propaganda, Russian—United States. | Mass media and
    propaganda. | Elections—Corrupt practices—United States. |
    Internet in political campaigns—United States. | Disinformation. |
    Fake news. | Social media—United States—History—
    21st century. | Hacking—Russia (Federation) | Political
    campaigns—United States—History—21st century. |
    United States—Foreign relations—Russia (Federation) | Russia
    (Federation)—Foreign relations—United States. |
    Trump, Donald, 1946– | Clinton, Hillary Rodham.
Classification: LCC E911 .B69 2020 | DDC 324.973/090512—dc23
LC record available at https://lccn.loc.gov/2019016498

ISBN: 978-0-367-20262-0 (hbk)
ISBN: 978-0-429-26053-7 (ebk)

Typeset in Times New Roman
by Apex CoVantage LLC

For Sofia, Dean, and Colette

Contents

Acknowledgments

I would like to thank the organizers and students of the OSHER program at California State University Channel Islands (CSUCI) and my colleagues and students in the Department of Communication at CSUCI for their continuing inspiration. I would like to extend my thanks to Professor Olga Baysha for her assistance in arranging my 2018 visit to the Higher School of Economics in Moscow, and to the faculty and students that I was privileged to address during that visit. Equally, I want to thank Professor Changchang Wu for his assistance in arranging my 2018 visit to the East China Normal University, Shanghai and to express my appreciation to the faculty and students whom I was privileged to address. In all three cases I am deeply grateful for the interest that was shown and the thoughtful questions that were put to me. I had the good fortune to travel to both Moscow and Shanghai in the company of my wife Leah without whose constant support, goodwill, and patience neither this book nor any other of my publications would have seen the light of day.

I am thankful to my series co-editor Andrew Hoskins for inviting me to join him in this exciting Routledge series a decade ago. As always, I am grateful to the consistently professional, supportive and wise guidance of Andrew Humphrys, senior editor of the Media, War and Security series. I express my deep appreciation to Andrew, his editorial assistant Bethany Lund-Yates, and to the entire Routledge team for the work they do.

Introduction

Perceptions of western mainstream media

In the spring of 2018 I addressed students, faculty, and public in universities of three countries – California State University Channel Islands (USA) (undergraduate students of the University's degree program and senior adults of its OSHER program), Higher School of Economics in Moscow (Russia), and the East China Normal University in Shanghai (China).

My presentations examined legacy and social media coverage of "fake news" and "RussiaGate" (2016–2019). In California as in Moscow and Shanghai I discerned that many listeners identified positively with western mainstream media, especially those of the USA and the UK (easily accessible in Russia and in China through the use of VPNs) contrasting these favorably with media of Russia and China. I surprised many with the view that western mainstream media are not dependably "safe" sources on topics that touch on matters of great sensitivity to the main centers of power, especially those with which we may associate the term "Washington Consensus," and its outlook on world affairs.

Brief history and prospective of fake news

President Donald Trump introduced a new chapter to a long history of fake news. Here was an establishment figure denigrating media for stories that he claimed were untrue and/or biased. Trump's complaints – petulant and self-serving as they often seemed – had some basis, since many so-called liberal media did indeed demonstrate bias against Trump, even if critics considered he had brought negative coverage upon himself.

"Fake news" is nothing new and has always raised concern. The term is itself 200 years old (Jankowski 2018). It is closely associated with a range of others, including "propaganda," disinformation," "information operations," "perception management," "public diplomacy," and "organized persuasive communication."

"Fake news" has been described as "patently false information (that) is intentionally presented in a phony but utterly believable 'news media' format in order to sway public opinion" (Macaray 2018). To illustrate, Macaray (ibid) recalled the 1934 California gubernatorial election contest between Republican incumbent Frank Merriman and Democratic challenger Upton Sinclair. Another candidate, one of America's richest men, was Ukrainian immigrant Louis B. Mayer, who had steered MGM to Hollywood dominance. Attacking Sinclair's popular campaign for "Ending Poverty in California," Mayer produced a series of faux newsreels. Looking authentic, these were shown in Californian theaters in order to discourage potential Sinclair voters. One newsreel depicted herds of desperate hoboes emerging from box-cars, whereupon they were interviewed by a faux journalist. Another showed a phony Russian declaring that he supported Sinclair because Sinclair's system worked so well in Russia.

British spy William Stephenson (possibly an inspiration for the fictional James Bond) was another example. He was assigned by Winston Churchill to manipulate the USA into WWII, to which some 80% of Americans in 1940 were opposed. Churchill sent multi-millionaire Stephenson to the US on a false diplomatic passport following Dunkirk. Stephenson's businesses included Shepperton Studios (movie production), and he had close ties to leading figures in the news business. He established a MI6 center in Rockefeller Center. This had two operational arms of which the British Information Service (BIS) was one, engaging in soft propaganda for entertainment media, including its own New Jersey radio station. BIS operative David Ogilvy was also assistant director to George Gallup, and skewed survey questions that could encourage the belief that US support for war was growing faster than it really was. BIS subsidized the Overseas News Agency, a branch of the Jewish Telegraph Agency, and fed manufactured stories, often couched within factual material, about German atrocities to the BIS-owned NJ radio station and similar outlets. Newspapers relayed this further. One story claimed the British had a new super-explosive for filling depth charges. It was printed on the front pages of all leading US newspapers known to be regularly monitored by Germany. Stephenson sent out rabble-rousers to spark riots among isolationist organizations, and provided funds to pro-interventionist organizations and candidates for political office. From Canada, he purportedly ran a network of 3,000 agents, counter-intelligence operatives, forgers, burglars, codebreakers, and killers.

Propaganda evolving

Of equal importance to such instances of dramatic fabrication is news coverage that misleads audiences by focusing on only certain issues, topics, sources etc. to the exclusion of others that are more significant for a thorough understanding of a given issue. The purpose is to induce a desired point of view, attitude or behavioral change. Perhaps more remarkable is evidence that has surfaced in the wake of "fake news" scandals of the Trump presidency, of original, more insidious methodologies in the realms of both propaganda distribution and production. An example is a cluster of techniques of "computational propaganda." This involves use of automation, algorithms, and big-data analytics to manipulate public life, (Howard and Woolley 2016). It encompasses

> fake news, spread of misinformation on social media platforms, illegal data harvesting and micro-profiling, exploitation of social media platforms for foreign influence operations, amplification of hate speech or harmful content through fake accounts of political bots, and clickbait content for optimized social media consumption.
>
> (Howard et al. 2018, p. 39)

Such methods have been attributed to a Russian propaganda and/or click-bait factory, The Internet Research Agency (IRA), but similar shenanigans closer to home featured in the techniques of Cambridge Analytica (US) to promote a variety of Republican candidates for office, and in those of its parent, Strategic Communications Laboratory (UK), which covertly intervened in the elections of dozens of countries worldwide.

An unsuspected depth and range of propaganda technique surfaced in the "Integrity Initiative" (II) scandal as revealed in documents released by hacking group Anonymous in late 2018. Founded in 2015 in cooperation with the Free University of Brussels, (VUB) II was a principal activity of the Institute for Statecraft and Governance (founded in 2006). Operating under close supervision from the UK's Foreign and Commonwealth Office it received over $3m a year from the British Army, UK Ministry of Defense, NATO, the US State Department, Lithuanian Ministry of Defense, and even Facebook. Set up to counter Russian disinformation, II appeared to act as a source of disinformation *against* Russia (although II claims that some hacked information may have been falsified), operating in over 13 countries. It set up covert networks or "clusters" of "experts" among politicians, journalists, academics, NGOs, and others for the purpose of disseminating influence, manipulation of the public sphere, and overt attacks on critics of UK government policies, even when these were members of the official opposition. II activity promoted hostility to ethnic Russian minorities in the Baltics and espoused Holocaust denial. In Spain it helped torpedo the appointment of Pedro Banos as Director of Spain's National Security Department on the bogus grounds that he was "pro-Kremlin." Many II staff, including its director, had military back-grounds (McKeigue, Miller et al. 2018).

Such efforts undermine the health of the public information environment. First and foremost, this study seeks to heighten awareness of the workings of contemporary official propaganda and warn against campaigns whose end purpose is contamination of public sphere discourse and that invite unprecedented planetary and species disruption.

Outline of the book

In Chapter 1 I identify three "portals" to the RussiaGate hall of mirrors: (1) allegations of Russian interference in the 2016 US election by means of manipulation of social media, (2) allegations of Russian hacking of servers and computers linked to the Democratic National Campaign, and (3) the inquiries of Special Counsel Robert Mueller into possible collusion between the Trump Campaign and Russia. The chapter examines the prior influence of two reports made public in January 2017. One was a dossier compiled by former MI6 agent Christopher Steele. This alleged collusion between Trump and the Trump campaign with the Russian government. Another was the Intelligence Community Assessment (ICA) which corroborated con-cerns of collusion.

Chapter 2 argues that a weakness of RussiaGate discourse was its nar-row understanding of "election meddling." There are many sources of non-transparent interference in elections. Examining only Russia, without reference to other sources was deceptive. Any list of major problems chal-lenging the integrity of the US electoral system would not prioritize Russia. Some allegations of Russian meddling were farcical: e.g. that Russia sowed "discord" in a country that is manifestly riven with social faultlines of long standing. The content of much of Russia's supposed interference was apo-litical and/or juvenile, as is consistent with clickbait and with commercial persuasion.

Chapter 3 defines key social media terms such as "bot," "troll," "sock-puppet," and "cyborg." It critiques charges of election meddling against Russia that appeared in intelligence and congressional reports as they con-cerned social media manipulation by Russia's IRA. A singular focus on the IRA to the exclusion of the machinations of Cambridge Analytica (US) and its British parent SCL, the wider phenomenon of bot and "influencer" manipulation, and the CIA and similar intelligence activity in social media manipulation is profoundly deceptive.

Chapter 4 argues that Cambridge Analytica is central to a critique of RussiaGate because (1) it exposes by contrast how low-key Russian efforts to "meddle" actually were (if indeed they *were*), while (2) revealing how elections throughout the world are subject to sophisticated and intelligence-linked psychological targeting operations that exploit the weaknesses of social and legacy media. Such operations function (3) principally at the service of conservative, neoliberal, or "radical right" interests, and (4) highlight inadequate self-regulation by social media whose business models depend on the privacy weaknesses of their networks to exploit big data for profit and incentivize application developers.

Social media and in particular Facebook were integral to the micro-targeting tactics of non-transparent political persuasion. Chapter 5 examines the business model underwriting of Facebook and other social media in terms not just of advertising *per se*, but of meta data banks made available directly or indirectly to corporate clients for financial, political, and other campaigns. A principal concern is whether in response to political criticism social media have shouldered the inappropriate responsibility for gate-keeping and fact-checking, sometimes in alliance with partisan institutions.

Chapter 6 finds footprints of intelligence agencies scarcely concealed behind various iterations of RussiaGate discourse, constituting contemporary forms of "deflective source propaganda," as in the media coverage of the UK Skripal affair in 2018. The British government asserted Russian responsibility long before it could have securely determined the nature or source of the poison or the manner in which it was deployed. The Skripal affair provides one in a long chain of pro-war NATO propaganda maneuvers against Russia, deflecting public attention away from possible ties between Skripal and the "Steele dossier."

Chapter 7 unpacks the tangle of issues surrounding alleged hacking (or leaking) by Russians (or others) of documents from the servers or computers of Hillary Clinton, the DNC, and the DNC's chairman, and its relevance to charges of "election meddling" by Russians in the 2016 US presidential election.

Chapter 8 argues that no adequate understanding of RussiaGate is possible without consideration of a much broader context than is usually supplied by mainstream media. This encompasses a history of hostile relations between the USA and the Soviet Union during the first Cold War, escalating hostility between Russia and the USA in a second Cold War that erupted with the accession of Vladimir Putin to the Russian presidency, and ultimately a geopolitical struggle for power across EurAsia, essential for the exercise of world hegemony. Four great nuclear powers in two alliances are implicated: USA/Europe and Russia/China. The threat of nuclear war remains real.

The 2019 RussiaGate report by Special Counsel Robert Mueller was published after this book entered production. Mueller's conclusions do not substantially impact the book's arguments.

1 Trump's campaign, the "Steele" dossier, and the intelligence community assessment

Trump and RussiaGate: main "portals"

President Trump's denunciations of what he called "fake news" amounted to wholesale condemnation of the RussiaGate narrative, much of which arose from charges of collusion between the Russian government, or its proxies, and Trump's 2016 presidential campaign. These charges were still being investigated at the time of writing by Special Counsel Robert Mueller, a former director of the FBI who was appointed in spring 2017. They play out in three main directions:

1 Alleged Russian interference in the election, in non-transparent ways, through social media, that included the use of anonymous or falsely identified websites and pages ("bots") and anonymous, paid-for social media commentary ("trolling") that can often be monitored, controlled, and programmed by artificial intelligence.

2 Alleged Russian hacking of the servers and/or individual computers of the Democratic National Campaign (DNC) and its partner group, the Democratic Congressional Campaign Committee and of the Chair of the DNC (John Podesta), the stealing of Hillary Clinton's private emails, and alleged Russian delivery of such hacked material to DCLeaks, Julian Assange, and WikiLeaks – in possible collusion with members of the Trump Campaign.

3 Alleged contacts between members of the Trump Campaign and Russian government officials or with Russians thought to have close ties to the Russian government. Interest in such meetings stems from widely publicized suspicions that the Trump Campaign invited or connived with Russian assistance in influencing the US voting electorate to vote for Trump, in possible return for the promise of a Trump Administration's support for a reduction in US sanctions on Russia and other benefits. These allegations embrace claims that Trump was a "Russian

asset" – as has been claimed by a former Director of Intelligence James Clapper, a former NSA official (Sheth 2017) and by the Steele Dossier (Bensinger et al 2017).

Robert Mueller and the Trump campaign

I shall not look in detail at the Special Counsel's charges or investigations targeting key Trump Campaign actors or their associates, such as the following: Michael Cohen, Jerome Corsi, Michael Flynn, Rick Gates, Rob Goldstone, Constantin Kilimnik, Paul Manafort, Carter Page, George Papadopoulos, Richard Pinedo, Roger Stone, Donald Trump, Jnr., and Alex Van der Zwaan.

Some of these people entertained a possibly surprising array of contacts with influential Russians, which in itself is neither criminal nor undesirable. The nature and extent of links of Trump or Trump administration figures to Russian businessmen, some of them possibly fitting the term "Mafiosi," some of them allegedly linked to Russian intelligence and to Russian oligarchs, has been the subject of numerous books and articles although some of these were arguably contaminated by a desire to damage Trump and rescue the tattered image of the Democratic Party following its electoral defeat (see Harding 2017; Unger 2018).

The significance of evidence against Trump campaigners is rarely clear-cut, encompassing activities that might have passed unscathed in other campaigns and relating to other countries. Trump National Security Adviser Michael Flynn had lied to federal investigators about his conversations with Russia's ambassador, Sergey Kislyak, during the Presidential transition. He asked Russia not to escalate tensions after President Obama imposed sanctions for alleged election meddling (Russia agreed to Flynn's request). He lied about conversations with Kislyak concerning Russia's UN vote on a resolution to condemn Israeli settlements in the West Bank. And he had lied about his lobbying work for the Turkish government (Leonnig et al 2017). What was it that was really important here: what he actually did? Or that he lied?

Mueller's supposed successes have often seemed irrelevant to the central issue of collusion. For example, Paul Manafort was convicted of financial fraud stemming from his earlier consultancy for the pro-Russian former leader of Ukraine. Manafort's associates Konstantin Kilimnik and Rick Gates were indicted for similar reasons. In November 2018, already in jail, Manafort's role was highlighted in a somewhat more relevant, though likely deceptive, way, when a *Guardian* story alleged that Manafort had visited Julian Assange at the Ecuadorian embassy in which Assange had taken refuge from possible extradition, including one such alleged visit in 2016.

The story was problematic: one author had long been thought close to MI6, sources were anonymous, and claims were based on intelligence said to have originated under the now right-wing administration of the government of Ecuador from Ecuador's intelligence service SENIAN. The proposal that somehow Manafort's visits had escaped detection by external security and press surveillance, and that his visits had not been logged by the Embassy yet information about them suddenly came to light in November 2018, was implausible and inexplicable (Harding and Collyns 2018). Subsequent revelations (debunked by Aaron Maté 2018) claimed that Manafort had passed polling data to his associate Kilimnik, whom some news media alleged was close to Russian intelligence (a claim Kilimnik denies and for which there is no evidence (Chalfant 2019).

Those who fell afoul of Mueller often made the mistake of lying to investigators – who presumably knew the real answers – even if there was no suggestion they had engaged in egregiously criminal behavior relevant to collusion. In January 2019 Mueller charged Roger Stone, Trump's political advisor, with obstruction, false statements, and witness tampering, and he accused Stone of being a conduit between the Trump campaign and WikiLeaks during the period when WikiLeaks released e-mails stolen from the DNC. *The New Yorker* noted that the charges stemmed not from the original acts themselves but from Stone's alleged lies about them (Davidson 2019). The principal issue was whether the timing of WikiLeaks's release of emails of DNC chair John Podesta (hacked or leaked from DNC computers) in October 2016 had been coordinated with the Trump Campaign with a view to neutralizing the Access Hollywood ("pussy-grabbing") video released on that same day and potentially damaging Trump's image. Did Roger Stone play any role in such coordination? Evidence that WikiLeaks's release was a response to Access Hollywood is thin (it could have been the reverse), as is evidence of Stone's involvement. Private emails from Julian Assange to Roger Stone appear to expressly deny any such relationship (McCarthy 2019).

Indictments and charges can be grossly contaminated by the politics of plea deals and maneuvers for leniency, presidential pardons, or other forms of judicial relief. By the time this book is published the special counsel's investigation may have established a robust case for collusion, one that can survive judicial or impeachment processes. At present, the published evidence falls short (Maté 2018a, b, c).

Trump sustained his ambition to "build" (i.e. lend his name to) a Trump Tower in Moscow well into the presidential campaign. His former lawyer, Michael Cohen, in November 2018 retracted earlier statements and alleged that negotiations continued at least up to May 2016 (other sources suggest much later). Cohen had agreed to visit Moscow on behalf of his client, but the trip never occurred, the tower did not get started, let alone built, no gift was given to Putin, and whether Trump's conflict of interest amounted to illegality is moot (Blake 2018). Cohen claimed he had briefed members of the President's family about the Tower, and had minimized Trump's role in pursuing a deal. Was any of this as damaging to Trump's credibility, electoral chances, and national interest as Cohen's role, whether or not under Trump's direct instructions, in paying off women who claimed to have had affairs with Trump and in securing a deal with a tabloid publisher that in return for payment the publisher would not publish such stories (Rutenberg and Protess 2018)?

Mueller's concerns therefore often appeared "legalistic" (e.g. to do with possible attempts to obstruct a legal investigation, to "cover up," or lying to special counsel investigators) rather than concerning matters of real substance pointing unequivocally to collusion with Russia for the purposes of securing electoral advantage. *Nation* writer Aaron Maté concluded that, after 5 guilty pleas, 20 indictments, and over 100 charges, "what's been revealed so far does not make a compelling brief for collusion" (Maté 2018). Russian affairs professor Stephen Cohen noted dismissively that "after all this time and frenzy, substantiated charges and indictments amount to little more than customary financial corruption on the part of the bipartisan top 2% and 'lying to the FBI,' the latter apparently open to interpretation as to what was actually said and perhaps involving entrapment" (Cohen 2018). Jason Ditz was equally scornful, denouncing RussiaGate as a "fraud, a setup, and really a criminal conspiracy to take down a sitting US President on the basis of a gigantic lie." Veteran investigative reporter Bob Woodward concluded that despite looking for over two years in researching his book *Fear*, he encountered no evidence of collusion nor espionage of the kind denominated by the label RussiaGate (Walsh 2018; Woodward 2018).

From a different perspective other commentators were incensed by what they saw as Democratic Party collusion with the intelligence establishment (including the British) to spy on and smear the Trump campaign, with help from Christopher Steele (ex-MI6), and Cambridge professor Stefan Halper (connected to MI6 and CIA: see Greenwald 2018). A reporter who had been briefed by Christopher Steele was Michael Issikoff, whose story on Steele's dossier aroused FBI interest. Former senator John McCain said he gave the dossier to James Comey, director of the FBI, after being briefed by former British ambassador to Russia Sir Andrew Wood (Haltiwanger 2018). The dossier (possibly leaked to Buzzfeed by an associate of McCain's – see Re 2018) and Issikoff's story provided justification for FBI's request for four FISA warrants to spy on Trump Campaign adviser Carter Page. Yet by December 2018, Issikoff told radio host John Ziegler that the Steele report had not been vindicated and that many of its allegations had yet to be supported (e.g. that Michael Cohen had traveled to Prague to coordinate with the Russians; the existence of the "pee tape" with which Russians were said to be blackmailing Trump; McGovern 2018d).

FBI source Professor Halper (Costa et al 2018) had allegedly "cultivated" an influential group that included George Papadopoulos (Trump campaign adviser in foreign affairs); Carter Page (Trump campaign adviser); Sir Richard Dearlove (former head of MI6); Joseph Mifsud – who introduced Papadopoulos to the idea that the Russians had incriminating evidence against Clinton (Papadopoulos was eventually jailed for one week for lying about the *timing* of his meeting with Mifsud); and Alexander Downer, formerly Australia's ambassador to the UK and who had notified the FBI of Papadopoulos's claims (Ditzd 2018; Ross 2018). By fall 2018, Papadopoulos was openly asserting that he had been set up by western intelligence agencies, including British (Cheney 2018b). British involvement in the 2016 US presidential election would not only have constituted illegal support to the Clinton campaign but would likely have far exceeded in magnitude and subterfuge the efforts attributed to Russia on behalf of Trump.

Suspicions of British involvement were compounded by reports in fall 2018 that MI6 struggled to prevent President Trump from releasing pages of FBI applications to wiretap Carter Page. M16 worried that sources might be compromised. Trump wanted declassification of FBI notes of its interview with Department of Justice employee Bruce Ohr and his wife. Along with Christopher Steele, the Ohrs were paid for information by Fusion GPS on behalf of the Democratic Party campaign. Bruce Ohr was twice demoted at the Department of Justice for evading exposure of his contacts with Fusion GPS (Durden 2018d, citing the *Daily Telegraph* among other sources).

Of interest is the arrest and pre-trial jailing in solitary confinement and later conviction of Marina Butina, charged in July 2018 of being a unregistered Russian agent who "under cover" of a Russian pro-gun advocacy group, had "infiltrated" the strongly Republican and, later, pro-Trump National Rifle Association and who had tried to arrange a meeting between candidate Donald Trump and Vladimir Putin. In a less hysteric perspective than that pertaining in 2018 her activities could reasonably have fallen under the description of transparent public relations or lobbying in the promotion of guns. She was charged by the Justice Department outside the purview of the Mueller investigation. Mueller had declined to investigate the case, and prior Senate Intelligence Committee scrutiny had not unearthed criminal activity (Bamford 2019). Butina had worked in association with Alexander Torshin, a longtime friend of the NRA who later served as the deputy head of the Russian central bank. Together, the two were suspected of attempting to establish a backdoor channel between the Trump campaign and the Russian government. At the time of writing, the FBI has not concluded its investigation into whether Torshin funneled money to the NRA in support of Trump. The story was denied by the NRA (who funded the Trump campaign by $30 million). It was Butina whom Trump called to put a question at a conference in Las Vegas in July 2015, prompting Trump to assert his interest in better relations with Russia (Prokop 2018b). Butina likely accepted a plea deal under considerable pressure when admitting guilt of failing to register as a foreign agent and being involved in an organized effort, backed by Russian officials, to open up unofficial lines of communication with influential Americans in the NRA and in the GOP and to win them over to the idea of Russia as a friend (Hornberger 2018a).

It is hardly strange that a country at the receiving end of sustained western efforts to undermine its geo-political security, sovereignty, and internal stability should seek friendlier relations with at least one of the major US political parties. A lengthy investigation by James Bamford (2019) who interviewed Butina many times concluded that the case against her was weak. The Butina case needs to be encompassed within an understanding of the full scope of lobbying of US politicians by overseas interests, a phenomenon so large it would deservedly dwarf RussiaGate. For example, it should be assessed in relation to the strong influence on US politics and public opinion of the America Israel Public Affairs Committee (AIPAC) on behalf of the government of Israel (Al Jazeera 2018; Mearsheimer and Walt 2017).

The "Steele dossier"

Responsible for the ensuing popularity of the term "fake news" was its use by President-elect Trump in criticizing CNN in January 2017 for its coverage that month of the "Steele Dossier" – then about to be published (without permission) by the online news site Buzzfeed. CNN reported that then FBI Director James Comey had briefed Trump about the dossier. (The FBI and CNN may have communicated with one another about CNN's disclosure; the likelihood of FBI leaks to the press played a role in Trump's firing of James Comey on May 9, 2017, and the later firing by Attorney General Jeff Sessions of the Deputy Director of the FBI, Andrew McCabe, on March 16, 2018). The briefing occurred on January 6, CNN reported it on January 8, and Buzzfeed published the dossier on January 10 (see Tracy 2017a; Davis 2018).

The Steele dossier alleged Trump connections and possible collusion with Russians, for the purpose of gaining advantage in the 2016 presidential election. The dossier was compiled by Orbis, a private investigation agency founded by British former MI6 agent Christopher Steele. Steele was also a FBI informant: FBI documents released to Congress in August 2018 showed that although Steele was cut off as a "Confidential Human Source" after he disclosed his relationship with the FBI to a third party, there were at least 11 FBI payments to Steele up to that time in 2016. He had been admonished for unknown reasons in February 2016 (Judicial Watch 2018). His company Orbis reportedly had links to a Russian oligarch Oleg Deripaska – with whom Paul Manafort, an associate of Trump, had connections in Ukraine (Mayer 2018). Steele at one time worked for MI6 in Moscow (1980s) and in the early 1990s headed up the Russia desk for MI6 in London. His report was contracted by Fusion GPS, which was, in turn, contracted by attorneys (Perkins Coie) working on behalf of the Democratic National Campaign and Hillary Clinton's presidential campaign. (Fusion GPS had initially been hired by a conservative website, the *Washington Free Beacon*, to conduct research on Republican candidates including Trump.) Among a number of astonishing allegations, the Steele dossier indicated that Trump was some kind of "Manchurian candidate" who had been identified as a possible candidate for high office by Russian authorities over several years, and was subsequently groomed by them. The report identified business and personal relations between Trump and various powerful Russians – the so-called oligarchs.

The main allegations (as yet unproven) of the Steele dossier were as follows (see Ewing 2018; Kessler 2018):

1   Trump had cooperated with Russian authorities for years. Russia "had been feeding Trump and his team valuable intelligence on his opponents," including Clinton, for "several years" before 2016. In exchange, Trump's team had fed the Kremlin intelligence on Russian oligarchs in the USA and their families "for at least eight years."

2   Trump was vulnerable to Russian blackmail on sexual matters.

3   There was a "conspiracy of cooperation" between Trump and Russia, managed by Trump adviser Paul Manafort, with Carter Page serving as intermediary until Manafort's firing in August 2016, after which point Trump's lawyer Michael Cohen was said to have played an increasingly large role in managing the "Kremlin relationship."

4   Trump's team was said to have known and approved of Russian plans to deliver emails, allegedly hacked by Russian intelligence from the servers and computers of the Democratic National Campaign and its chairman John Podesta, to WikiLeaks, and offered the Russians policy concessions in exchange.

5   Trump adviser Carter Page was said to have played a key role in the conspiracy. Carter Page had "conceived and promoted" the idea that the DNC emails to WikiLeaks should be leaked during the Democratic convention, "to swing supporters of Bernie Sanders away from Hillary Clinton and across from Trump."

6   Trump lawyer Michael Cohen was said to have played a key role in a conspiracy to cover up and limit damage arising from Manafort's

work for the regime of Viktor Yanukovych in Ukraine (deposed with US assistance in 2013) and in efforts to prevent exposure of the full details of Trump's relationship with Russia.

Craig Murray, a former British ambassador, ridiculed the Steele report. He asked how a small, private outfit could have persuaded senior Russian spies to talk about a five-year-old "Manchurian candidate conspiracy" without the knowledge of Russian or US intelligence. Steele's contacts seemed dated and Murray speculated whether this might reflect the putative influence of Sergei Skripal in providing data for the dossier (Murray 2018a; Keefer 2017). Former *Guardian* journalist Luke Harding, who reported for the paper from Moscow for several years, suggested in his book that several Russian spies were actually liquidated as a result of their talking to Steele, but he offered little by way of hard evidence and is a problematic source, given his reportedly pro-MI6 and anti-Putin record (Harding 2017; Murray 2018b; Sputnik 2017).

Russia specialist Stephen Cohen found the dossier unconvincing, not least on account of "an abundance of factual errors, inconsistencies, outright contradictions, and, equally important, information purportedly from secret Kremlin sources but that had already been published in open Russian or other media" (Cohen 2018). Cohen ridiculed Steele's allegations that Putin had personally "ordered" and "directed" the RussiaGate operation on behalf of Trump, and the supposed motives that have been variously assigned to Putin for doing so. Cohen considered Steele had outrageously underestimated the established rationality of the Russian president.

The Steele dossier had nothing to say about a history of arguably Russia-friendly policies by the Obama administration or possible links between Russians and the Democratic Party. Putin referred in 2018 to some $400 million in illegally earned profits funneled to the Clinton campaign by associates of American-born British financier Bill Browder – at one time the largest foreign portfolio investor in Russia. Putin claimed that the scheme involved members of the US intelligence community. Browder made billions in Russia during the 1990s. In December 2017, a Moscow court sentenced Browder in absentia to nine years in prison for tax fraud, while he was also found guilty of tax evasion in a separate 2013 case. Putin accused Browder's associates of illegally earning over $1.5 billion without paying Russian taxes, before sending $400 million to Clinton (Durden 2018c; Schwirtz and Barry 2018).

Intelligence Community Assessment (ICA)

The ICE report was signed off by the Director for National Intelligence, James Clapper, and published on January 5, 2017. It raised concern about

Russian influence on the 2016 elections in social media and Russian hacking (Office of the Director of National Intelligence 2017; Mayer 2018). Although Buzzfeed's publication of the Steele dossier occurred a few days later, on January 10, the Steele dossier or information based on it had been in circulation in security circles before Steele formally submitted the report in October 2016 (Barrett and Hamburger 2018). The July 2018 summary report of the Senate Intelligence inquiry into Russian meddling specifically claimed that the Steele dossier had not been used by the ICA because the ICA team considered it "unverified."

The ICA report (ODNI 2017) concluded that the president of Russia, Vladimir V. Putin, personally "ordered an influence campaign in 2016 aimed at the U.S. presidential election," and evolved from seeking to "denigrate" Hillary Clinton to developing "a clear preference for President-elect Trump." It talked of covert Russian cyber activities and "trolling," and accused Russian intelligence agencies of hacking the DNC and accessing electoral boards. Much of ICA's discussion focused not on sinister, anonymous sources but on highly public coverage by state-directed international television channel RT, doubtless as biased towards the interests of Russia as Voice of America was biased in favor of the USA. RT was judged by one relevant academic study to have been only a "moderately visible" site in the USA during this period even if its content was frequently republished by right-wing site *Infowars* (Benkler et al 2018).

Hillary Clinton and many mainstream media lauded the ICA report as representing carefully researched conclusions of the entire, 17-agency US intelligence establishment. The DNI's director James Clapper and CIA director John Brennan testified in May that the ICA voiced the conclusions of a small team likely hand-picked by Clapper, from only three of the agencies (CIA, FBI, and NSA). Technically such an "assessment" contains no guarantees of accuracy. A consensus of all 17 agencies must involve some form of a National Intelligence Estimate (or NIE) (Parry 2017). Former US envoy to Moscow James Matlock observed that, of these three agencies, two had no responsibility nor necessarily any competence to judge foreign intentions and that "what should have struck any congressperson or reporter was that the procedure Clapper followed was the same as that used in 2003 to produce the report falsely claiming that Saddam Hussein had retained stocks of weapons of mass destruction" (Matlock 2018). Further he noted the unusual inclusion of the FBI and was perplexed that Clapper did not call on the National Intelligence Council, the Defense Intelligence Agency (DIA), or the Bureau of Intelligence and Research (INR) of the State Department which, Matlock says, had different views to that of the ICA.

The group hand-picked from the DNI, FBI, CIA, and NSA declared (with the exception of the NSA, which was less convinced) "high confidence" that Putin had ordered an influence campaign. Yet the term "high confidence" was qualified on p. 13 of the report – which did not contain any actual evidence – as a term that "does not imply that the assessment is a fact or a certainty; such judgments might be wrong. . . . Judgments are not intended to imply that we have proof that show something to be a fact" (ODNI 2017). Given the records of the agency directors involved, we may speculate whether they were appalled by indications copiously confirmed by Trump throughout the campaign that Trump was inclined towards peaceful relations with Russia, a policy direction seemingly at odds with the course of Washington policy concerning Russia since the accession of Vladimir Putin to the Russian Presidency in 2000. (For an early critique of the ICA, see Goldstein 2018). The ICA was rejected by the House Permanent Select Committee on Intelligence (HPSCI) in March 2018 on the grounds that any influence exerted by Russia did not specifically favor Trump. Democrats on the committee issued a near-100-page dissenting "minority views" comment (and further HPSCI investigations were anticipated after Democrats secured a House majority in mid-term elections in November 2018). The Senate Intelligence Committee (2018) took the opposite view in its subsequent report in May, its summary report focusing on allegations that Russian hackers had breached the electoral infrastructure in as many as 20 states, although no attempt was claimed to have been made to change voter tallies or electorate registration information. The Snowden NSA leaks in 2013 would suggest that this kind of hacking is also well within the capability and possibly the practice of the US espionage and surveillance agencies.

Hillary Clinton and the FBI

In June 2018, the Office of the Inspector General of the US Department of Justice published its report concerning the conduct of FBI investigations into whether Hillary Clinton had committed offenses in handling of classified material during her period as Secretary of State (Office of the Inspector General 2018). FBI Director James Comey publicly announced on July 5, 2016, that although Clinton had been "extremely careless" (a term chosen on reasoned grounds to distinguish the gravity of Clinton's actions from "gross negligence," which would more likely have been prosecuted), no reasonable prosecutor would charge her with a criminal offense. In letters to Congress on October 28 and November 6, 2016, Comey partly reversed this position when he announced that the FBI had reopened its investigation in the wake of the discovery of thousands of Clinton emails, possibly containing classified materials, on the computer of the husband of one of Clinton's aides, a vice-chair of Clinton's 2016 presidential campaign, Huma Abedin.

The husband was Anthony Weiner, then under investigation for "sexting" (a charge to which he pleaded guilty in May 2017).

Comey's public announcements raised questions as to his and/or the FBI's neutrality with respect to the presidential contest, and as to whether the FBI applied different standards to the Clinton investigation than it did to its still secret investigations into "RussiaGate." The Justice report did unearth evidence of anti-Trump sentiment among five FBI employees involved in either or both the Clinton and the Trump investigations and, in one case (concerning the email correspondence between FBI counterintelligence official Peter Strzok and his mistress FBI attorney Lisa Page), found evidence of possible willingness to obstruct the course of justice for the purpose of preventing a Trump electoral victory. The report concluded that this "raised a cloud" over the FBI investigation and FBI credibility. Strzok was fired from the FBI in August 2018.

The FBI Director's public statements were neither unconsidered nor senseless; nor does it seem that they were the result of political bias. Comey appeared to have substantial reasons for his decisions to act unilaterally, with little or no direct consultation either with the Attorney General, Loretta Lynch, or with the Department of Justice. But the report concluded that he violated Departmental "practice and protocol," demonstrated "extraordinary and insubordinate" behavior, made a "serious error of judgment," and engaged in *ad hoc* decision-making based on personal views.

There were other concerns. The report encountered considerable evidence of a "cultural attitude" permissive of unauthorized contact between FBI employees and media reporters, extending to the receipt of benefits from reporters. This raised "profound concerns." The wife of then assistant director (Andrew McCabe) of the FBI's Washington Field Office had received backing from Hillary Clinton in the race for the Virginia State Senate in 2015. McCabe became Deputy Director of the FBI in February 2016, was active in the supervision of the Clinton investigations until he recused himself on November 1, 2016, and has since referenced some level of FBI consideration in spring 2018 as to whether Trump might be removed from office (Goldman and Haag 2019). A former Assistant Attorney General who participated in Clinton-investigation communications had sought to obtain employment for his son with the Clinton campaign.

Subsequent events did not eradicate doubts as to impartiality of investigations into Trump Campaign collusion with Russia. Timing of indictments by special counsel Robert Mueller (a former FBI director) against 12 Russians accused of hacking the DNC in 2016, occurring within a few days of Trump's meeting with Putin in Helsinki on July 16, 2018, could have seemed to undermine Trump's credibility and boost the RussiaGate narrative favored by the Democrats, defense and intelligence establishments, and thus bring pressure on Trump to conform. Controversy over the FBI's FISA court applications to spy on Page in October 2016 was sharpened in July 2018 when the agency consented to deliver over 400 pages (albeit heavily redacted) of evidence to Congress. FBI concerns about Page's links with senior Russian government figures and oligarchs while he worked for the Trump Campaign were sparked by the by-now partly discredited Steele dossier. The FISA application acknowledged the dossier and that it was paid for by opponents to the Trump candidacy. Evidence by FBI attorney Lisa Page to a joint committee of the House of Representatives in July 2018 as to the meaning of messages to her from Peter Strzok raised the possibility that senior FBI officials had even lost confidence in the substance of the collusion narrative by spring 2017, in turn indicating that everything since that time had been politically, not legally motivated (McGovern 2018c).

One possible reading of the confluence in early 2017 of the ICA, publication of the Steele dossier (well known by this time to the FBI, and paid for by the Democratic Campaign), and escalating media criticism of the announcements during the campaign of FBI Director James Comey as these may have impacted (unfavorably) the Clinton campaign, was that the security establishment of the USA, with the strong backing of "liberal media," reacting to their own surprise with the outcome of the election, were now doing all they could to discredit or to "contain" Trump, largely through the manufacture of the RussiaGate narrative.

Such suspicions were amplified by revelations concerning the presence of FBI sources inside or close to the Trump Campaign, possibly from a point in time prior to the official opening of the FBI's investigation into Russian "meddling." Congressional committees pressured the FBI for the release of relevant documentation. By June 2018 several thousand pages were in the process of being supplied (Cheney 2018a). Further releases were expected pertaining to uses by the FBI of the Steele dossier as a pretext for obtaining FISA surveillance warrants.

2 "Election meddling" and the health of US democracy

RussiaGate as fake news misrepresenting the scope of "election meddling"

In January 2017 Trump derided CNN reporting of the soon-to-be-published Steele dossier as "Fake News!" CNN was merely doing its job in giving advance notice of the publication of significant allegations that had been treated with some seriousness by elements of the security establishment – damaging as these clearly were to the President. Whether CNN lived up to standard journalistic expectations by means of critical follow-up research into the Steele dossier and the Intelligence Community Assessment is another matter (see Dowling 2017).

I argue that the ensuing saga of RussiaGate, still raging to the time of writing, is itself an example of "fake news." Why? Because much of it was based on over-assertive allegations that have yet to be proven, some of which were false or questionable (as I shall show in subsequent chapters), yet often assumed by media to be dependable. Second, it was misleading. The attention that this discourse gave RussiaGate suggested that the events in question were more significant, unusual, and important than they really were. For example:

1   Actual instances of Russian "collusion" and "meddling" were rela-tively insignificant when compared to western-based subversion of social media by political, intelligence, and commercial agencies – of which Cambridge Analytica and its parent company SCL were among the most notorious, not least because of their close association with leading figures in the Trump Campaign and, through SCL, with the intelligence, defense, and fossil fuel industries of both the USA and the UK. In other words, exploitation of social media data – generally without the consent of users – for the purposes of precisely tailored, covert electoral propaganda has been a routine practice for the USA

and some of its close allies for many years and arguably exceeds comparable Russian efforts (Ahmed 2017; Cadwalladr 2018; Rosenberg et al 2018; Dyer 2018). Chapter 3 picks up on these considerations.

2   RussiaGate discourse suggested that were one to be really concerned about the health of democracy in the USA, one would begin with worrying about the Russians. In point of fact, I shall argue here, the Russians should have appeared very low down the list of any such preoccupations.

Challenges to US democracy

There are many challenges to the integrity of democratic process in the USA, none of which has anything to do with Russians. Challenges include the vulnerability of voting machines to hacking – this has been demonstrated many times. Such concerns have inspired many anguished articles and editorials, even in the *New York Times* (e.g. see Zetter 2018a) for well over a decade. As late as November 2018, *CBS News* reported that tens of thousands of voting machines in the USA were vulnerable to hacking. Security researchers for years had demonstrated their flaws. In 2017, a technology professor from the University of Copenhagen was able to penetrate an Advanced Voting Solutions machine in about 90 minutes. The attackers had the potentiality to alter voting data. A group of hackers in 2018 was able to crack one in 15 minutes (Patterson 2018). Data transmission was also vulnerable where unencrypted results went from voting machine into a piece of electronics carrying it to the central counting place. An expert interviewed by *Scientific American* in 2018 noted that only about 79% of votes across the country were recorded on a piece of paper. Without a paper trail it was impossible to perform a rigorous audit (Schwartz 2018).

McClatchy in August 2018 reported critical vulnerabilities with the Georgia electronic voting system prior to the 2016 presidential elections, further evidence of weaknesses of electronic voting as generally implemented in many parts of the USA at that time (Gordon et al 2018). *Motherboard* reporter Kim Zetter noted in July 2018 that the nation's top voting machine maker E&S had admitted in a letter to a federal lawmaker that the company installed remote-access software on election-management systems it had sold over a period of six years, raising questions about the security of those systems and the integrity of elections that were conducted with them. Although the particular problem had been resolved, it illustrated a potential for future weakness in electronic voting. The company said that that it had "provided pcAnywhere remote connection software . . . to a small number of customers between 2000 and 2006" (note that as of May 5, 2014, pcAnywhere was discontinued with no replacement offering). At least 60%

of ballots cast in the USA in 2006 were tabulated on ES&S election-management systems. The company stopped installing pcAnywhere in December 2007 after the Election Assistance Commission, which oversees the federal testing and certification of US election systems, released new voting system standards. Election-management systems contain software that is used to program all the voting machines used in some counties; the systems also tabulate final results aggregated from voting machines.

A critical vulnerability in pcAnywhere at that time allowed an attacker to seize control of a system that had the software installed on it, without needing to authenticate themselves to the system with a password. Researchers with the security firm Rapid7 scanned the Internet for any computers that were online and had pcAnywhere installed on them, and found nearly 150,000 were configured in a way that would allow direct access. A long-time expert on voting machines confirmed that other companies routinely installed remote-access software during this period. As late as 2011, pcAnywhere was still being used on at least one ES&S customer's election-management system in Venango County, Pennsylvania (Zetter 2018b).

In the run-up to the 2018 mid-term elections, millions of Americans were expected to vote on old, hack-prone digital machines that produced no paper trail. The *Washington Post* in 2018 reported that 95% of digital security experts surveyed by The Cybersecurity 202 said that state election systems were not sufficiently protected against cyber threats. Several experts said that state voter registration databases were particularly vulnerable and made an appealing target for attackers who wanted to sow confusion and undermine confidence in the voting process (whether domestic or foreign). "The 'back end' systems, used by states and counties for voter registration and counting ballots, were equally critical to election security, and these systems were often connected, directly or indirectly, to the Internet" (Hawkins 2018). The reality was that states were understaffed, underfunded, and too heavily reliant on election-system vendors for securing their own systems. State balloting systems were diverse and decentralized, administered by some 3,000 counties, making it difficult for malicious actors to uniformly attack voting infrastructure on a vast scale, but there remained plenty of incentive for more targeted attacks at critically important local levels (ibid).

There have been multiple efforts to "suppress" voting (especially in areas significantly populated by people of color). These have been exacerbated by the Supreme Court's 2013 decision in *Shelby v. Holder*. This undermined the Voting Rights Act of 1965 on the grounds that while there was still evidence of discrimination it was not sufficient to warrant the "extraordinary" remediation measures that the act imposed on the states of the former Confederacy (Cobb 2018). Thirty-three states have implemented voter identification laws which bar up to 6% of the population from voting (London 2018). There have been multiple cases of citizens being struck off voting lists either because they have committed felonies or, even more outrageously, because they have names that are similar to people who have committed felonies (Palast 2017).

Voting has been and continues to be suppressed in many other ways. These include the following: allowing state attorney generals to retain charge of election procedures when they or their parties are also candidates in those elections, requiring that signatures on ballots exactly match signatures on file, prohibitions against transportation to early voting venues on the grounds of "political activity," reductions in the available hours of voting; denial of extra time in the event of long queues of people still wanting to vote, and failure to supply adequate numbers of functioning voting machines; requirements for additional documentation to establish identity (Gumbel 2017). A Supreme Court decision in June 2018 allowed states to purge voter rolls of those who had not recently voted and who had not responded to requests for confirmation of address (Sherman 2018).

Evidence from whistleblower Christopher Wylie indicated that Cambridge Analytica, answering to senior advisor and right-wing alternative journalist Steven Bannon, helped engage in social media propaganda designed to depress the Black vote in critical "rust-belt" constituencies that might otherwise have fallen to Hillary Clinton (O'Sullivan and Griffin 2018b), using techniques more commonly ascribed to Russia's IRA.

Of broader concern has been "Citizens United" legislation passed under the administration of President Barak Obama that virtually opened up the US political process to unlimited, anonymous "big money" from any part of the globe, often channeled through PACS (political action committees) or super PACs that are not directly linked to political parties but serve partisan goals (Biersack 2018). For the mid-term 2018 elections, overall, "dark money" groups funded about a third of the TV ads airing in House races and almost half of those in Senate races. Put in other terms, two out of every three ads came from an outside spending group. More than $260 million of such money had been spent on nearly 400,000 TV ads between January 1, 2017 and May 3, 2018, in races for House, Senate, and governor, according to a report by the Wesleyan Media Project and the Center for Responsive Politics. Typically, the groups were run as 501(c)(4) social welfare organizations that are not supposed to be political in nature. Such groups do not have to disclose their donors. They tend to spend heavily during the long run-up to an election but are only required to report their advertisements to the FEC *30 days before* a primary or *60 days before* the general election. They can mention candidates and issues, and run supporting or oppositional ads (Ambroz 2018).

An assessment in July 2018 calculated that secret donors had financed more than four out of every ten television ads up to that point in time for the 2018 congressional elections. Two groups affiliated with the right-wing billionaire Koch brothers accounted for more than one quarter of the advertising for congressional races from January 1 to July 8, 2018, accounting for approximately 96,500 of the 386,000 television spots dedicated to the races. Conservative-leaning groups accounted for four out of the five biggest secret-money advertisers (Schouten 2018).

All this was in addition to traditional sources of lobbying from overseas interests, among them Israel, Saudi Arabia, and UAE whose foreign policies are highly questionable from the standpoint of world peace yet which are known to have tried to exert influence on US elections. Pro-Israel lobbying accounted for over $4 million in 2016 (Sultan 2017). John Mearsheimer and Stephen Walt (2008) in their book *The Israel Lobby and US Foreign Policy*, described the lobby as a "loose coalition of individuals and organizations who actively work to steer US foreign policy in a pro-Israel direction." The coalition includes the American Israel Public Affairs Committee (AIPAC) a US-based pro-Israel lobbying group that in 2018 spent $1.75m to promote pro-Israel policies. Noam Chomsky told Andrew Buncomb in July 2018 that for anyone interested in foreign interference in US elections:

> Whatever the Russians may have done barely counts or weighs in the balance as compared with what another state does, openly, brazenly and with enormous support. I mean, even to the point where the prime minister of Israel, Netanyahu, goes directly to Congress, without even informing the president, and speaks to Congress, with overwhelming applause, to try to undermine the president's policies – what happened with Obama and Netanyahu in 2015.
>
> (Buncomb 2018)

More globally, one can point to the overwhelming role of money in US elections, money that predominantly represents corporate and plutocratic power. Corporations spent roughly $3 billion lobbying the government in 2017 alone. Six billion dollars was spent influencing the 2016 elections. This spending took place in a society that was becoming increasingly and egregiously unequal. As noted by the *World Socialist Web Site* two of the country's richest people – Jeff Bezos and Bill Gates – possessed almost the same amount of wealth as the poorest half of the population. The richest 5% of the population owned 67% of the wealth. The poorest 60% of the population owned 1% of the wealth. The wealthiest Americans lived an average of 20 years longer than the poorest Americans. Seventy percent of Americans had less than $1,000 in savings. There were 554,000 homeless people on a given night (London 2018).

Then there is the problem of the gerrymandering of congressional constituencies so as to produce highly predictable electoral outcomes. In the

early 21st century the outcome of 94% of House races is a foregone conclusion. In 408 of the 435 House elections, one party is favored to win with
chances that exceed 90%. The Republicans have better than a 90% chance
of winning in 231 races and the Democrats have a better than 90% chance
of winning in 177. It is profoundly problematic that Congress can have an
approval rating of 12.9% (RCP average) yet have so many noncompetitive
House races (Taylor 2014). Ballot restrictions make it impossible for third
parties to challenge the domination of the Democratic and Republican parties (London 2018). An even more fundamental problem therefore is the
domain of electoral procedure, the rules and laws that make it difficult
for third parties to secure a place in the otherwise two-party dominated
system.

The USA trails behind most developed countries in voter turnout.
According to the Pew Research Center, nearly 56% of the US voting-age
population cast ballots in the 2016 presidential election. This was slightly
better than in 2012 but less than in the record year of 2008. The 2016 figures
placed the USA behind most of its peers in the Organization for Economic
Cooperation and Development (OECD) at 26 out of 32 (Desilver 2018).
There is low voting turnout of many sections of the electorate, particularly
among those of color and the poor (CNN 2016).

The US Republican Party, in the event of its losing elections for state
governorship, has taken to passing legislation in ensuing "lame duck" periods of transition that is designed to limit the power of incoming Democratic
governors: in other words, making it impossible for the winners of elections to bring about the changes that voters presumably voted for. Measures
by Republican legislators to strip power from incoming executive branch
Democrats were taken in North Carolina (2016) and Wisconsin and Michigan in 2018 (Quinton 2018).

The overblown fuss about Russian "meddling" in US elections farcically
ignores the substantial history of US "meddling" in the elections of other
countries. Mainstream media have rarely afforded RussiaGate discourse
adequate historical context in this respect. Public attention is thus distracted
from the substantial history of US "meddling" (which I don't have the space
to go into here) – sometimes egregiously through invasion and occupation,
as in Iraq 2003, when the pretexts for invasion were totally fabricated,
and these fabrications were lapped up uncritically by mainstream media
(see Blum 2004; Privy Counsellors 2016). Dov Levin of Carnegie Mellon
studied instances of foreign election meddling between 1945 and 2000 and
concluded that the USA was responsible for 69% of the cases he found
(Shane 2018). In an effort to oust Venezuela's President, Nicholas Maduro,
the Trump administration even identified the head of the opposition as the
country's legitimate leader in January 2019.

In addition, there is a strong right-wing tilt to US "meddling in the elections" of other countries. Such interventions do not only involve unfortunate "Third World" countries such as Iran (where the CIA and MI6 deposed democratically elected Prime Minister Mohammed Mossadegh in 1953), Indonesia (where western intelligence contributed to the end of the Sukarno regime at the cost of a million lives in 1967), and Chile (where CIA tactics effectively deposed Salvador Allende's democratically elected government in 1973 in favor of the military dictator Augusto Pinochet). They were also rampant in "allied" "First World" countries including France, Germany, Greece, Italy, and Spain and also in the UK and Australia. There is an extensive literature on all these events. Blum (2004) provides a useful summary. A history of over 100 years of western meddling in Islamic nations or manipulation of Islamic groups has been chronicled among others by Curtis (2012) and Davidson (2016). In Greece, Blum reported that the government was virtually run by the CIA up to and during rule by the Military Junta that it helped install from 1967 to 1974 (Blum 2004). Consider also the (disputed) case of the conspiracy between MI5, the CIA, and leading figures in the British press to unseat Labour Party Prime Minister Harold Wilson in the 1960s. First there was a conspiracy to prepare a military *coup d'etat* that would have made Lord Mountbatten – cousin to the Queen and the last viceroy of India – head of the government. When this did not gain sufficient support, a sex scandal was fabricated involving Wilson's secretary Marcia Williams (later Lady Falkender) perhaps culminating in Wilson's 1976 resignation (Moran 2013). There was another conspiracy (by Australian intelligence, MI6, and the CIA) to overthrow Australian Prime Minister Geoff Whitlam in 1975. As Pilger notes, "Whitlam ended his nation's colonial servility. He abolished royal patronage, moved Australia towards the Non-Aligned Movement, supported 'zones of peace' and opposed nuclear weapons testing." He also wanted to reduce the role of the CIA and its use of Australia as a global center for CIA espionage. The CIA had infiltrated the Australian political and trade union elite and referred to the governor-general of Australia, Sir John Kerr, as "our man Kerr."

> On 11 November – the day Whitlam was to inform parliament about the secret CIA presence in Australia – he was summoned by Kerr. Invoking archaic vice-regal "reserve powers," Kerr sacked the democratically elected prime minister. The "Whitlam problem" was solved, and Australian politics never recovered, nor the nation its true independence.
>
> (Pilger 2014)

This "right-wing" tilt of "election meddling" has continued, as the analysis of Cambridge Analytica (Ahmed 2017) confirms.

Concerns about alleged Russia meddling continued into the lead-up to the 2018 mid-term elections in the USA, with evidence provided in July 2018 by Facebook and the FBI to the effect that they had identified evidence of attempts to "divide America," possibly linked to Russia. Once again, the value of any such evidence without a much broader sweep of all of the possible ways in which any interests or parties from anywhere might attempt to influence US (or other) elections was less than it might seem (though very useful to the continuation of anti-Trump RussiaGate propaganda). The alleged attempts at divisiveness (for example, calls to unite the Right, or for the abolition of the department of Immigration and Customs Enforcement [ICE]) overlapped with identifiable legitimate campaigns; they had credible, logical connections with actual divisions within the electorate and therefore a legitimate place within the "marketplace of ideas," whatever their provenance. In short, RussiaGate's trope of "election meddling" has been defined much too narrowly at the service of special interests, and mainstream media coverage largely followed suit.

3 "Bots" and "trolls"

Introduction and summary

"Bots" have been defined as "fully automated accounts or scripts that simply share, tweet, or retweet news headlines, with or without links, retweet other accounts, or exhibit similarly simple actions in high volumes with minimal human supervision" (Benkler et al 2018, pp 9–10). Numerous allegations linked large numbers of 2016 campaign-related bots to Russian agencies. Harvard team Benkler et al (2018) protest that "finding bots is hard" and "finding Russian bots is harder." It is unclear when any given account can be deemed a bot or when a network of accounts can be considered to be coordinated, nor does the mere presence of an army of bots determine whether their content has been utilized by other sources.

The same source prefers the term "sockpuppet" to the more popular "troll." Sockpuppet "usually refers to fully human accounts that pretend to be people they are not." Whereas in American usage the term "troll" has several meanings, in Russia it refers to "human participants paid to intervene in the online conversation to shape it in favor of whoever is paying them." "Cyborgs" are accounts or groups of accounts (whose sources are) paid to post repeatedly, and who use scripts and supervised automation (Benkler et al 2018). One authority (Coles 2018) found that bots were pushing fake news to make stories go "viral" by sharing them among "sockpuppets" on social media. Coles cited a Texas A&M University experiment that created gibberish-spewing Twitter accounts. These soon had thousands of followers that were, in fact, bots.

Accusing Russia

In this section I shall revisit the charges made by the ICA of January 2017 (ODNI 2017) and by Special Counsel Robert Mueller's indictments of March 2018, to the effect that the IRA, among other Russian actors, was guilty of meddling in the 2016 US presidential election, principally by

(1) taking out advertisements – anonymously – on social media, whose purpose was to "sow discord," (2) organizing and promoting rallies, (3) establishing large numbers of "bots" which were not transparently identified with their Russian patrons and whose purpose was to sway opinion in ways that would influence the election, (4) feeding "troll" commentary on third party social media pages or websites, and (5) traveling to the USA under false pretenses to collect intelligence for these interventions (U.S. District Court of the District of Columbia 2018).

A critic of these indictments writing in July 2018 speculated that Mueller had likely expected that indicted parties would not appear in court, not being bound by US law nor having anything to gain by participating. Contrary to expectation, a few did send their lawyers and demanded discovery, which would have forced Mueller to reveal the evidence he had against them. "Finding his own indictments riddled with errors – one of the companies named didn't even exist at the time of the election – Mueller quietly backpedaled. Score one for the Russians" (Buyniski 2018).

I shall argue (1) that evidence that these allegedly Russian activities were designed to favor Trump is not strong, and has actually been rejected by the (GOP-dominated) House Intelligence Committee (HPSCI 2018) though accepted by a subsequent Senate Select Committee on Intelligence and by reports commissioned by that Committee; (2) that the amount of money available to the IRA for such activities ($1.25 million a month) was modest (Bloomberg News 2018); (3) that the amount spent on social media advertising ($100,000 in the case of Facebook between June 2015 and May 2017 – spent by 470 fake accounts on a total of 3,000 ads – and possibly an additional $50,000 for 2,200 ads from sources that "might have originated in Russia") was miniscule (total digital advertising expenditure in the 2016 election cycle was $1.4 billion [Associated Press 2018a]); and (4) that the impact of any such advertising would have likely been slight.

Relatively few "events" (rallies) (5) were organized or promoted by the IRA. It is unlikely that more than a very small number of these – not more than eight and probably only three – actually occurred, and even then it is unlikely that they attracted large numbers (Moon of Alabama 2018b). Such small-scale impact suggests not a political motivation, which would have required far greater investment, but a click-bait operation of some kind, or an experiment.

The IRA perhaps contributed (6) towards a "bubble" tendency wherein existing predispositions are confirmed. Some research indicates that the majority of social media users who followed the Russian ads and other messages were already following pro-Trump right-wing sites such as Breitbart News and Fox (Benkler, Faris, Roberts, and Zuckerman, 2018, ibid). A contrasting study found that people who used Facebook for news were more likely to view both pro- and counter-attitudinal news in each wave, and that counter-attitudinal news exposure increased over time, which resulted in depolarization (Beam et al 2017).

Social media influences should be located within the broader context of overall media influence to include the influence of partisan, advocative, ideological and propagandistic legacy media, both US and international, that might be said to have had an impact on the US elections. These would include Fox News, for example, or the tabloid AMI-owned National Enquirer which explicitly collaborated with the Trump Campaign, providing drafts of its stories for pre-publication approval and allowing Donald Trump to preview stories about his rival (Stern 2018). Other candidates would include MSNBC, or, of course, RT. RT was even mentioned in the ICA assessment as an alien influence and RT in the USA has since been required to register as a foreign agent. But RT is a public, transparent source, much of its international reporting meets standards similar to those of other international broadcasters, and it comports to a long-established tradition of overseas foreign broadcasts that fall into the category of "soft power" that are disseminated by almost every major nation. "Though legacy media do harness digital distribution channels to spread content, come election time they remain the most active and influential sources of information" (Cunningham 2018a).

False or misleading American social media accounts were certainly far more in evidence in the media consumption of American political activists and supporters than Russian. The vulnerability of social media to fraud is part of the broader context – including corporate, political, and criminal activity, often involving bots, trolls, false or anonymous identities that rage across many different kinds of campaign to bolster the popularity of stars, products and political positions (Holm 2014). Less than 60% of web traffic is actually human (Read 2018). A report by PlainSite (a legal data non-profit owned by Aaron Greenspan, who unsuccessfully pursued a claim that he had originated the idea of Facebook) charged that fake accounts likely exceed 50% of the Facebook network (Herman 2019).

Covert micro-targeting and Cambridge Analytica

The idea of vulnerability to fraud of social media generally is a convenient segue to Cambridge Analytica (in the process of liquidation at the time of writing, soon to be reborn by a similar cast of players as Emerdata [Murdock 2018]). Analytica was founded by Trump adviser Steve Bannon, with money from Board directors and billionaires Robert Mercer and his daughters – all friends to President Trump – and very close to its parent British company SCL (Cadwalladr 2018; Ahmed 2017). Consideration of Analytica invites a review of companies similar to it that trade in big data and micro-targeting (while not forgetting more traditional public relations companies such as Bell Pottinger – now defunct – Hill and Knowlton or the Rendon group that have received political and military payments to construct war propaganda).

When we are talking about Cambridge Analytica and SCL we are talking about the following:

1   Allegations of fraudulent persuasion whose sponsors and origins are unknown to their targets.
2   Massive exploitation of personal social media data, for which permission was not explicitly given, for electoral propaganda – e.g. to influence the outcome of Congressional races in 2014, the "Brexit" vote in Britain in 2016, and of the 2016 US presidential election (CA and SCL denied they used psychographic micro-targeting for the 2016 election). The company reportedly used a self-destruct email server to erase its digital history (Morse, citing Channel 4 Television 2018).
3   Subversion of or collusion with social media corporations whose business models rest on advertising and the building and sale of mass audiences, offering methods of access that enable precise targeting of audiences by advertisers.
4   Election manipulation on a global scale. A March 2018 television documentary about SCL and the claims that it made to potential clients seeking assistance in election campaigning disclosed evidence of potential bribery, slander, and honey traps (Channel 4 News 2018).
5   Involvement of the "security establishment" (Ahmed 2017), as detailed later.
6   There was a Russian connection via Alexandr Kogan, a Cambridge University psychologist with links to the University of Saint Petersburg who reportedly worked on Russian government-funded research projects investigating Internet use (Cadwalladr and Graham-Harrison 2018). SCL was reported to have pitched to Russia's Lukoil, indicative of warm relations between SCL and the fossil fuel industry. SCL had previously worked with the oil and gas industry to defuse popular concerns about fracking (Dyer 2018) and Lukoil may have had a similar interest.
7   Kogan's data combined Facebook user information with personality features his company collected from data that the users contributed in response to personality quizzes, and which were collected via Facebook's then-permissive "Graph API" – the interface through which third parties interacted with Facebook's platform (Hindman 2018).

Facebook declared in 2018 that it had ended this kind of privileged access to user data several years' previously, but a December 2018 investigation published by the *New York Times* reported that Facebook had given Micro-soft, Amazon, Spotify, and others far greater access to people's data than previously disclosed and for longer. Up to 150 client organizations were implicated and all such deals were active in 2017. Facebook had effectively exempted these companies from usual privacy rules, potentially affecting 2.2 billion users. Microsoft's Bing search engine had permission to see the names of virtually all its users' friends without their consent. Netflix and Spotify had the ability to read users' private messages. Yahoo was allowed to view streams of friends' posts and Apple devices were enabled to conceal that they were asking for data, making it impossible for users to disable sharing (Dance et al 2018).

These scandals increased pressure for greater regulation of social media. They opened the door to greater censorship (e.g. both through physical cen-sors, of which there were several tens of thousands employed by social media at the close of 2018; and through algorithms) and encouraged social media to act as gatekeepers of "acceptable" information, in the process boosting the perceived legitimacy of established mainstream media, at the considerable expense of alternative but legitimate media sites (Gourarie 2018; Johnstone 2018a; *Washington Post* 2018). Apparent justification was conveniently supplied in late 2016 by "ProporNot" – an entity granted anonymity by the *Washington Post* (Timberg 2016) and whose principal purpose, according to research by George Eliason (2018), was to smear websites critical of the RussiaGate narrative. Eliason's exposure implicated a chain of neo-liberal propagandists starting with Michael Weiss – National Security Analyst for CNN, and editor in chief of *The Interpreter* (a product of pro-NATO think tank or propaganda agency, the Atlantic Council, and closely associated both with Ukrainian Intelligence and the US Broadcast-ing Board of Governors – VoA, RFE/RL). ProporNot's fabricated charges were exploited to justify support for measures that suppress genuine politi-cal dissent. Not only did the business shenanigans of social media giants likely do far more to corrupt the information environment of Americans than any alleged Russian malfeasance, they also provided those who had previously done the most to push the RussiaGate narrative new opportunity to make life difficult for information sources critical of that narrative.

The Internet Research Agency

The stated extent of Russian meddling was less dramatic or impressive than generally claimed by US sources especially with respect to numbers of websites; number, reach, and content of advertisements; and number of political events arranged and of people who actually attended them. Much of the alleged Russian activity (over 50%) continued beyond the 2016 election (Associated Press 2018b).

IRA may have been a clickbait operation primarily. There has been continuing lack of clarity about IRA. Some details emerged in western mainstream media well before the election – so secrecy was not the organization's strong hand. Its owner, Yevgeniy Viktorivich Prigozhin, was described by the Mueller investigation as a Russian restaurateur and caterer widely known as "Putin's chef" on account of his hosting of Putin's state dinners with foreign dignitaries (Bloomberg 2018). Two of Prigozhin's companies, Concord Catering and Concord Management and Consulting, were alleged to have had Russian government contracts. Elsewhere, Prigozhin has been described as a hamburger magnate who established this "troll" outfit as a company promotion and to contest the claims of rival operators (Levintova 2017). None of this constitutes adequate, authentic information about the company's real purposes or nature.

In November 2016, Facebook claimed to have discovered that Russian operatives had aggressively pushed DNC leaks and propaganda on Facebook (Hartmann 2018). In September 2017, Facebook disclosed that beginning in June 2015, Russians had paid Facebook $100,000 to run 3,000 "divisive" ads (Associated Press 2018b). Contrasted with what we know of corporate advertising and political expenditure on social media this is a small amount of money, and the number of advertisements is modest compared to the hundreds of thousands of tailored ads that were routinely run through Cambridge Analytica in support for the Trump Campaign or, before then, for campaigns such as the one it ran for John Bolton's super PAC (Lewis 2018). Some of the accounts most thought to have contributed to social divisiveness (i.e. divisions already well and truly established in the USA) attracted a significant number of followers. Accounting for a strong majority of these followers, *Secured Borders*, *Blacktivist*, *Heart of Texas*, and *Being Patriotic* reached nearly a million between them (Wells 2017) – a trivial figure when set against the sum total of followers of all Facebook sites that may have aligned themselves to one issue or another relevant to the 2016 election.

The activities of the IRA were hardly secret. They had been subject to reporting in public media since 2015. Much of what appeared in the Mueller indictment about the IRA in February 2018 had been already revealed by the Russian media outlet RBC in 2017 (Chen 2018) giving the lie to another favorite western mainstream media trope about Russia, namely that there is no critical press in Russia. The agency had been identified as a source of pro-Russian propaganda during the Ukraine crisis by John Sipher (former CIA station chief; Sipher 2017).

In assessing the activities of the IRA more realistically we should take the following into account:

- The operation had a monthly budget of $1.25m for its entire global operations (of which the USA was only a part; Bloomberg News 2018).
- The February 2018 Mueller indictment did not mention Russian Intelligence involvement, only the apparent owner, Mr. Prigozhin, the hot dog vendor who appears to have started IRA as a troll farm to counter negative reviews of his hamburgers (Levintova 2017). In its early days, IRA's activity was domestically oriented, in Russian, much of it focused on making Putin look good (Graff 2018). Several people listed in the February Mueller indictment had not worked for IRA since 2014 (Taylor 2018).
- The majority (56%) of the Facebook ads paid for by the IRA had nothing to do with the election, and 25% of the ads were never shown to any user (Feldman 2017). Vice-President of Facebook Ads, Rob Goldman, claimed that most of the Russian ad spending occurred *after* the election (Marketwatch 2018).
- Facebook claimed in Congressional testimony that the posts from IRA pages represented a tiny fraction of the overall content on Facebook – about four-thousandths of 1% (0.004%) of content in News Feed, or approximately 1 out of 23,000 pieces of content (Byers 2017). Even this was likely an over-estimate.
- Only a small proportion of the ads or posts received significant attention. Facebook estimated that roughly 126 million people might have been *exposed* to material originating from the IRA between January 2015 and August 2017 (not the ten-week election period). The original Facebook source for this – Facebook's General Counsel, Colin Stretch, in testimony to the Senate Judiciary Committee in October 2017 – was expressing a theoretical possibility, not an established fact (Porter 2018). But there is little information as to how many saw, digested, or even thought about the ads (Feldman 2017). Facebook's Vice-President for News Feed, Adam Moseni, calculated that Facebook subscribers typically read only 10% of the stories that Facebook puts into their news feed each day. On the basis of these considerations, Porter calculated, the Russian-sourced Facebook posts represented 0.0000000024 of the total Facebook content during the two years.
- Twitter found 3,814 accounts it believed to have originated with the Russian troll group, and sent emails to 677,775 users who had inadvertently followed or interacted with content made by the trolls. These were small numbers in the context of the ten million suspected bot or spam accounts that Twitter identified and challenged in May 2018, up from the 3.2 million estimated in September 2017)(Burnett 2018).

- 80,000 posts attributed by Facebook to the IRA (and they may or may not have been election related) during 2015–2017, were engulfed in a social media universe of 33 trillion Facebook posts (Porter 2018). Only an estimated 29 million Facebook users would have received at least one such story – the figure of 126 million (earlier) was calculated on the assumption that the original 29 million shared the stories.
- Some ads appeared to discourage African Americans from voting, and some supported third party candidates (such as Jill Stein of the Green Party; Morris 2018) possibly in order to divide voters. Depressed turn-out fatally hurt Clinton in "rust-belt" states of Wisconsin, Michigan, and Pennsylvania, but the IRA ad campaign did not go out of its way to target these areas. If Clinton had run a more effective campaign, she would have much more likely have succeeded in the rust-belt. She did not give enough attention to the rust-belt states and what attention she did give came too late (Brownstein 2016). African American voters were already targeted by voter-reduction tactics across America including disfranchisement of felons, the false data-matching of voter rolls with lists of felons, insufficient voter machines in African American neighborhoods, inflexibility in polling hours, and suspension of previous day voting opportunities. There was also evidence of Cambridge Analytica involvement in voter suppression campaigns (O'Sullivan and Griffin 2018b).
- There is no evidence of anyone being "enflamed" as a result of whatever the IRA may or may not have done. One of the Russian Facebook groups, Black Matters, had an event page for a protest in New York City the weekend *after* the election, which it promoted with an ad. More than 16,700 people signed up to attend on the event page, while 33,000 more listed themselves as interested (Glaser 2018). For many of the rallies that the IRA is said to have organized, few people showed up or none at all. Three of the total of eight rallies occurred after the election; the first two may never have taken place, and the fourth (flash mobs in Florida) got minimal response or was undocumented. Nobody forced anyone to go to any of these rallies (Devoe 2018). When the influence of IRA and its rallies are compared to the successful effort by the Trump Campaign to prompt massive attendance at his rallies (Sullivan and Johnson 2016) their significance evaporates.
- The Russians are alleged to have sought "discord" – but the discord was indisputably there and much of it related to very real and ugly scandals that would have roused anger in any community, including several recent, notorious police killings of African Americans. Max Fisher and Amanda Taub in the *New York Times* argued that the notion that any Russian effort could match the power of existing partisan

polarization was fanciful. The false information and political ads that the Russians were accused of spreading could have rung true only to those predisposed to suspect the worst (Fisher and Taub 2018). Russian efforts were indicators – not drivers – of how widely Americans had polarized. And in large measure the polarization was racial (ibid).

- Since Facebook's algorithm is structured to show a user material that the user already agrees with, the impact of IRA ads would have been limited (Griffith 2017). The people most likely to consume fake news were already hyper-partisan, and false news was only a small fraction of their media consumption (Taub and Fisher 2018).
- Plausibly, many of the IRA ads were clickbait and perhaps all of them were (Real News Network 2018). Facebook executive Rob Goldman has opined that swaying the election was not the main goal. Most of the groups behind the problematic pages had clear financial motives and were not likely to have been connected to a foreign government (Maté 2018). The special counsel's investigation itself identified IRA as a commercial marketing scheme. IRA strategies have been found consistent with the techniques used in digital marketing. The IRA sold "promotions and advertisements" on its pages; these generally sold in the $25–50 range. It even sold merchandise. It has been argued that IRA's contents focused on themes that took the least effort to create while attracting a maximum readership for the benefit of advertisers, and that contents that highlight the plight or concerns of marginal-ized populations – by definition under-represented or negatively repre-sented in mainstream media – might be particularly drawn to such sites (Moon of Alabama 2018a).
- Some of the ads, according to one commentator, were simply absurd and could not possibly have had any predictive outcome (Madrigal 2018).
- Giraldi queried whether, apart from money laundering aspects and pos-sible visa fraud, any of the so-called IRA activity was actually illegal – especially if the people behind it all were NOT agents of the Russian government (Giraldi 2018).
- Following investigations, parallel claims of Russian interference in French and German elections have been disavowed by social media authorities (Associated Press 2017; Schwirtz 2017). As for claims of Russian interference in the British Brexit of 2017, Facebook found only three ads, bought for less than a dollar (Burgess 2017). A greater weight of evidence pointed towards the possibility of Trump campaign influence on Brexit through Steve Bannon in whose capacity as vice-president of Cambridge Analytica was party to talks with members of Leave.EU prior to the 2015 public launch of its campaign for a ref-erendum. Talks embraced a possible role for Cambridge Analytica in

raising money for Brexit in America. Foreign financial contributions to elections are illegal in both Britain and the USA (Meyer 2018).

The wilder world of bots

Earlier allegations about Russian bots often emerged from an agency, Hamilton 68, funded by the German Marshall Fund. The Fund was headed at the time of writing by Karen Donfried, a former operative for the National Intelligence Council. Executive vice-president was a former Assistant Secretary of Defence. The Fund's Alliance for Securing Democracy has been described as a collection of Democrats and neocons funded in part by NATO and USAID (Urie 2018). Hamilton 68 tracked a secret set of bots and then claimed that the bots had been steering public narratives online. The organization acknowledged that the methodology was in its infancy, still a blunt instrument needing human intervention. A co-founder of Hamilton 68, Clint Watts, called the RussiaGate narrative "overdone." The 600 Twitter counts monitored by Hamilton 68, he conceded, were not necessarily bots, and probably not even Russian; some were "legitimately passionate people" (Ditz 2018a). A comparable effort, Robhat Labs, claimed to identify bots that disseminated political propaganda, but critics complained that it too had sometimes classified real human social media accounts as bots (Smiley 2017).

RussiaGate discourse suggests that *only* Russians could be motivated to produce large numbers of deceptively or confusingly-sourced bots – a wild improbability. An AP report in August 2018 cited illustrative evidence of a "dedicated band of Trump supporters who tweet and retweet *Keep America Great* messages thousands of times a day" (Burnett 2018). They had exploited so-called Twitter rooms, which operated using the group messaging function. One member had participated in ten such rooms, each with 50 members who were invited in once they had attracted a certain number of followers. Her tweets were seen by 51,000 followers and then retweeted by dozens more people, each of whom might have 50,000+ more followers. Many of these supporters were actually identified as "bots" by social media, and their accounts suspended.

Several companies specialize in discovering bots in order to determine if "influencers" are buying fake followers. Some bots use the personal information of real people without their knowledge for the purpose of "influencing." "Influencers" mainly get paid according to the numbers of followers they can claim. People with two million or more followers can charge $40,000 per post. Fake "followers" often come from other countries. One source estimated that an average of 16.4% of the followers on Instagram were fraudulent.

In short, the "bot" phenomenon is infinitely larger than and overshadows the question of Russian influence on the 2016 presidential election (Maheshwari 2018). A *New York Times* investigation in 2018 found that although inflation of views violated (Google's) YouTube's terms of service, Google searches turned up hundreds of sites offering "fast" and "easy" ways to increase a video's count by five hundred, five thousand or even five million. The sites, offering views for just pennies each, also appeared in Google search ads. Nearly all of the purchases, made for videos not associated with the news organization, were fulfilled within two weeks (Keller 2018).

Academic research

Academic evaluations of alleged Russian meddling have been mixed or contradictory. Patrick Warren and Darren Linvill of Clemson University (Timberg and Harris 2018) amassed an archive of three million tweets they attributed to Russian operatives between February 2014 and May 2018. They identified periods of intense tweeting activity that appeared calibrated to respond to changes in the information environment and that prefigured major news developments such as the Wikileaks publication of DNC emails. As many as 20 million Twitter clients may have been reached by such tweets. Hundreds of accounts targeted different demographics. Their content varied widely, and included a heavy dose of political commentary. The relevance of the archive amassed by the researchers was questionable, since it extended back to a period well before it was known that Trump would be the Republican candidate and well beyond the 2016 elections. Not all the accounts studied were necessarily "trolls." Not all the accounts necessarily contained "disinformation," although failure to disclose the true origin of a communication may itself constitute misinformation. In May–June 2017 Twitter suspended 70 million accounts representing an amount equal to 20% of Twitter's 336 million active monthly users, but the purge mostly applied to inactive users, or bot accounts, instead of the revenue-generating accounts of real people (Durden 2018b).

An empirical persuasion study by University of Pennsylvania communications researcher Kathleen Hall Jamieson (2018) concluded that Russian activity very likely delivered a victory for Trump. Jamieson appeared to interpret the 126 million Facebook users said to have been exposed to Russian ads as hard evidence rather than merely an informed estimate. She was impressed by how the Russian ads appeared to successfully target African Americans, discouraging this normally pro-Democratic demographic from voting by smearing Clinton's image or using such smears to encourage voter participation among veterans and church goers who might otherwise have wavered in their support for Trump. Jamieson argued that the Russian campaign was duplicitous because sources were not transparent. Coupled with Russian participation (presumed, not proven) in Wikileaks's release of hacked emails from Clinton's campaign manager, the Russians had succeeded in promoting the view that Clinton was not forthright, leading to an unusual decline in support for Clinton during the presidential debates.

Jamieson depended on a number of questionable premises: for example, that voters might have acted differently had the Wikileaks's release of Podesta emails not served to distract voters from the "grabbing pussy" or "Access Hollywood" scandal exposing Trump's misogyny, or had the emails of Trump campaign managers also been hacked.

More significantly, Mueller's second round of indictments against Russians in 2018 included the allegation that Russian hackers had acquired the Clinton campaign's data analysis and voter-turnout models. Jamieson calculated that this enabled the IRA to target Clinton defectors in key swing states, including Michigan, Wisconsin, and Pennsylvania. If only 12% of third party voters in those states had switched their votes to Clinton, she would have won.

Further, Jamieson considered that the behavior of the FBI's James Comey in reopening the criminal investigation into Clinton's use of her private email server just before the election might have been influenced by allegedly forged Russian evidence that Comey's boss, Loretta Lynch, would go easy on Clinton over Bill Clinton's questionable meeting with Lynch at Arizona Airport in June. This argument focused on the second of Comey's three statements on this matter but downplayed Comey's third statement which cleared Clinton again.

By contrast, a Harvard study of press coverage (Benkler et al 2018) discovered that the most read and widely circulated stories were about Clinton's private server, not about the DNC and Podesta email accounts, and that coverage of the private server scandal originated long before the election in March 2015. Press coverage of the DNC email scandal was relatively brief. The authors contested the claim that coverage of the Podesta emails had diverted attention from the Trumpian "Access Hollywood" scandal. When the Podesta emails did receive attention, it was because right-wing media outlets had spun outrageous and false stories that were not, in fact, based on the emails.

The Harvard team did not question the presumption that Russian agents had in fact hacked the DNC emails and used fake email accounts, but they deemed Russian efforts miniscule when compared to the influence of Fox News and "the insular media ecosystem it anchors." The Russians merely jumped on their bandwagon, achieving influence only when right-wing media picked up on and embellished their accounts. American right-wing media did the "heavy lifting" of origination and distribution.

The authors dismissed the notion that Russia was culpable for Clinton's loss. Instead, they argued, a conservative US media network had excelled the Democratic Party in cunning. Unlike their counterparts on the right, left-wing media provided consumers more diversity, more often sourced to professional journalists who were closer to the facts and who were quicker to resort to fact-checking sources. More important still, in the right-wing media ecosystem, 40% of Trump voters said that Fox News was their primary source of election news, while only 7% credited social media or Facebook in particular. Support for Trump was especially high among demographics that had least exposure to social media or the Internet.

Jamieson's argument was challenged by at least two other academic sources. One of these (Sides et al 2018) argued that Russia was not a major factor in the outcome of the election. Trump's exploitation of divisive race, gender, religion, and ethnicity was the main factor accounting for his win. The University of Michigan's Brendon Nyhan (2018) argued that most forms of political persuasion have little impact and that the number of Russian messages was very small in relation to the total. He estimated that although 2.1 million Tweets had been attributed to Russia these constituted only 1% of all election-related tweets, and 0.5% of all views of such tweets.

The Senate Select Committee on Intelligence in December 2018 released two commissioned, supposedly "independent" reports that inspired Democratic Party leaders and mainstream media to confirm a high degree of Russian meddling. The reports actually added little to the debate and in some ways weakened the arguments for Russian meddling or its significance. One of them, *The Tactics and Tropes of the I.R.A.*, came from a think tank, New Knowledge. This cited hundreds of social media posts on Facebook as evidence of IRA sowing of discord. Credibility of the report was almost immediately shot down by reports that New Knowledge had contributed to a false flag operation designed to influence the Alabama state election in 2017 by making it appear that Russia was conducting a Twitter campaign to back the Republican candidate. In its "Project Birmingham," New Knowledge created fake Facebook pages to attract conservative voters, created 1,000 Twitter accounts with Russian names, promoted an obscure Republican to rival the leading Republican candidate (Roy Moore), attempted to artificially inflate click rates on anti-Moore news stories and schemed to link the Moore campaign to thousands of Russian accounts that suddenly began following Moore on Twitter (Shane and Blinder 2018).

New Knowledge was closely connected to US intelligence agencies. Its CEO, Johnathan Morgan was formerly adviser to the US State Department and had previously worked for DARPA. Co-founder Ryan Fox was with the NSA for 15 years and was also an analyst for the US Joint Special Operation Command. A $1.9 million grant from Moonshots Capital kept New

Knowledge afloat. Founders of Moonshots Capital were Kelly Perdew, an ex-US army intelligence officer, and Craig Cummings, an ex-US army intelligence officer serving in support of the NSA (see Morrow 2018b and Damon 2018d).

The second of the Senate reports came from Oxford University's Computational Propaganda Research Project. It was based on data supplied by social media firms to the Senate Select Committee on Intelligence. The report concluded that Russian activity had reached "tens of millions" in the period 2013–2018; that 30 million users had shared IRA posts 2015–2017; that organic posts were more influential than advertisements; and that the IRA activity was designed to polarize the USA, discourage electoral participation by African Americans, Latinos, or Hispanics and spread sensationalist, conspiratorial, and other misinformation (Howard et al 2018).

But social media firms have not been transparent as to their methods for determining Russian accounts. Most of the researched activity (54%) occurred *after* the 2016 election when it substantially increased, peaking in April 2017. Very little material actually pertained to the 2016 campaign as such. Explicitly political material represented only 11% of all content attributed to the IRA, and 33% of user engagement. Posts were minimally about the candidates. A few successful pages accounted for a very high percentage of all views. The top 20 most "liked" pages received 99% of all audience engagement, shares and likes; and the top 20 ad campaigns received most attention and absorbed the majority of IRA spending.

Many posts contained mistakes such as use of Russian phone carriers or IP addresses for Saint Petersburg in account metadata for user profiles. This might suggest the leaving of deliberate footprints by western agencies pretending to be Russian, or it might suggest a level of carelessness from an agency that was more interested in money than credibility.

Johnstone (2018d) has complained that the Oxford report's insistence that the IRA was seeking to discourage minorities from voting betrays an infantalization of American voters that presumes they are unable to think for themselves and unduly influenced by content much of which (the majority) was non-political and puerile. The report focused only on alleged Russian propaganda to the exclusion of all other sources. The amounts spent were extremely small. IRA ad spending on Facebook 2015 to 2017 amounted to $73,711 of which only $46,000 was spent before the election (less than previous sources had claimed). Ad expenditure data did not reveal any sophisticated focus on swing states. Only $3,102 was spent on a combination of 54 ads that focused on Wisconsin, 36 ads on Michigan, and 25 ads on Pennsylvania – in contrast to the 152 ads bought for the safely Democratic New York in the same time period. Overall ad spending represented a mere 0.05% of the $81 million that had been spent on Facebook ads by Clinton and Trump campaigns combined. A further $4,700 was spent on Google in 2016. In short, IRA activity was miniscule. Given that 126 million US users were served with an IRA story 2015–2017, this would represent a ratio of one IRA post to 23,000 other pieces of content (Maté 2018).

CIA meddling

The Russians did not invent trolls. CIA troll activities have been public since at least 2011. In the *Guardian* on March 17, 2011, Nick Fielding and Ian Cobain revealed a US spy operation that manipulated social media. A Californian corporation (Ntrepid) was awarded a US CentCom contract to develop an "online personal management service," part of "Operation Earnet Voice" designed to allow one US serviceman or woman to control up to 10 separate identities based all over the world. The journalists noted that critics of the program would likely "complain that it will allow the US military to create a false consensus in online conversations, crowd out unwelcome opinions and smother commentaries or reports that do not correspond with its own objectives."

The program would create online identities – known as "sockpuppets." The CentCom contract stipulated that false identities should not be capable of being discovered by sophisticated adversaries. A CentCom spokesperson said the purpose was to counter violent extremist and enemy propaganda outside the USA. None of the interventions would be in English, nor would US-based websites such as Facebook or Twitter be targeted. Each controller would have one virtual private server located in the USA and others appearing to be outside the USA to give the impression that the fake personas were real people located in different parts of the world (Fielding and Cobain 2011).

In 2014 the *Guardian* revealed a £60,000 UK Ministry of Defence project called *Full Spectrum Targeting* (Coles 2018) to identify and co-opt influential individuals, control channels of information and destroy targets based on morale rather than military necessity, and a parallel £310,000 *Cognitive and Behaviour Concepts of Cyber Activities* project.

In September 2018, WikiLeaks published 8,760 classified CIA files revealing its secret hacking arsenal, with details of "malware, viruses, trojans, weaponized 'zero day' exploits, malware remote control systems and associated documentation." The leaks indicated that a CIA unit used the American Consulate General Office in Frankfurt am Main as a base for hacking attacks on Europe, China, and the Middle East. The documents revealed that the CIA could remotely activate certain Samsung smart televisions equipped with cameras and microphones to turn them into bugs. Further, if the CIA had hacked a cell phone, it could then bypass encryption methods used by popular chat. The CIA had the ability to conduct false flag attacks using malware stolen from other nations (DW 2017). An analyst wrote:

> The documents revealed by Edward Snowden prove that the US and UK intelligence services have specialized and sophisticated departments that are dedicated to manipulating information that circulates on the internet to change the direction of public opinion. For example, the Joint Threat Research Intelligence Group of the Government Communications Headquarters (GCHQ), a British intelligence agency, has a mission and scope that includes the use of "dirty tricks" to destroy, negate, degrade and run over its enemies.
>
> (Zero 2018)

Examination of RussiaGate as fake news and other recent instances of fake news related in some way to RussiaGate (the Skripals, chemical weapons in Dhouma, the Iran nuclear "threat") raise the question of whether, even if the basic strategies of propaganda remain fairly constant (e.g. demonization, simplification, symbolization by means of deceit, incentivization, or coercion) the tactics of propaganda have grown far more sophisticated in the digital and social media age, requiring new approaches to propaganda identification and dissection. Far from any such new era in propaganda tactics originating from Russia, this chapter has suggested that the USA and its major western allies are just as or even more compelling agencies of interest.

4   Cambridge Analytica and Strategic Communications Laboratories (SCL)

All about Cambridge Analytica

Cambridge Analytica (now liquidated, along with its parent company Strategic Communications Laboratories, SCL) was the target of many inquiries 2018–2019. Study of Cambridge Analytica is essential to making sense of RussiaGate as "fake news" because (1) it demonstrates, by comparison, how low-key the Russian efforts to "meddle" in the US election actually were (if indeed they *were*), while (2) revealing the considerable extent to which elections throughout the world are subject to sophisticated and intelligence-linked psychological targeting and other operations that exploit the weaknesses of social and legacy media, almost always (3) at the service of conservative, neoliberal or "radical right" interests, and (4) exposing inadequate self-regulation by social media whose business models depend precisely on the privacy weaknesses of their networks to allow data exploitation for profit and to incentivize application developers (Joseph 2018).

Facebook suspended the accounts of Analytica and its contractor Alexandr Kogan in 2018, prohibiting their purchase of ads or running clients' Facebook pages. Facebook claimed the companies failed to delete the data they insisted they had destroyed in 2015 and which Analytica had acquired from Kogan (Shieber 2018): 270,000 users downloaded Kogan's application, yielding access via friends' networks to what were first estimated at 50 million accounts, of which 30 million were usable. Facebook founder Mark Zuckerberg later said that 87 million accounts (principally US) were involved in the Analytica scandal, and even that two billion accounts around the world had been contaminated by the facility – which it claimed it had now removed – that had allowed users to enter phone numbers or email addresses into Facebook's search tool to find other people, and that allowed malicious actors to scrape public profile information (Frier 2018).

The software Kogan sold to Analytica matched personality data with Facebook profile information as the basis for demographic micro-targeting of persuasive messages. It used a Facebook loophole later closed (but apparently active for some companies through 2017) allowing developers of Facebook applications not only to see the data of people who downloaded their applications, but also that of their friends (Stahl 2018). Analytica claimed it had never used the data for Trump's election campaign, and the GOP seemed to support that claim (although Analytica had used such data for micro-targeting and psychographics in other Republican campaigns, including one for John Bolton's super Pac; Lee et al 2018).

Whistleblower Christopher Wylie described Analytica as an "arsenal of weapons in a culture war" (Rosenberg et al 2018). Propaganda expert Jonathan Albright called it a "weaponized AI Propaganda Machine" (Anderson and Horvath 2017). Press attention to Analytica early in 2018 culminated in its liquidation (and that of its parent) – surprising, because the story (reported in the *Guardian* by Carole Cadwalladr as early as February 2017) was not new. There was something odd about the timing of the 2018 flurry, perhaps related to the House Permanent Intelligence Committee (HPIC) 2018 decision to close their investigation into RussiaGate and to the HPIC's dismissive attitude to ICA of January 2017, claiming to have "identified significant intelligence tradecraft failings that undermine confidence in the ICA judgments regarding Russian President Vladimir Putin's strategic objectives for disrupting the U.S. election" (Herb 2018), a view categorically rejected by the summary Senate equivalent, published in July 2018. Did the demonization of Analytica serve to keep a flame beneath allegations of mischievous exploitation of social media that would reflect badly on Trump? Democrats, then a minority on the House Intelligence Committee, charged that the Republican investigation was intended to help protect Trump, not uncover collusion, and they questioned the Republicans' findings about the ICA report and their call for an inquiry into that assessment.

Analytica's parent was SCL – whose regular clients included the UK Ministry of Defense and US Department of Defense, and whose divisions included SCL Elections, the one that gave birth to Analytica. SCL's expertise was "psyops" – seeking to change people's minds not through persuasion but through "informational dominance," including rumor, disinformation, and fake news. It regarded Information Operations as the fifth dimension of the battle-space of modern military strategy, after land, sea, air, and space. By 2017 SCL had deployed its techniques in 200 elections around the world, mostly in undeveloped democracies (Ahmed 2018b).

SCL was a "UK Ministry of Defense contractor which retains close ties to the British FCO and other elements of the UK political and financial establishment" (Ahmed 2018b). The British Foreign Office executive agency, Wilton Park, in 2017 invited SCL Group to "speak about how the use of data in the 2016 Presidential election could be applied in the British government's diplomatic and foreign policy agenda." SCL Elections's CEO Mark Turnbull had previous "psyops" experience on behalf of USA and UK occupations of Iraq and Afghanistan. Working for PR firm Bell Pottinger (now defunct) he oversaw a $540m US Department of Defense contract that included the creation and distribution of fake al-Qaeda videos in Iraq (including "beheading" videos). A former SCL website boasted of an "extensive worldwide track record and enquiries (that) can be directed through any British High Commission or Embassy." SCL was long classified by the Ministry of Defense as a "List X: contractor" – i.e. one that worked on contracts requiring it to hold classified information at their own premises or other specific sites (Ahmed 2018b).

Leading personalities behind SCL were identified by Liam O'Hare (2018). Head of SCL was Nigel Oakes, an old Etonian with links to the British royal family. In 1992, Oakes described his work as using the "same techniques as Aristotle and Hitler. . . . We appeal to people on an emotional level to get them to agree on a functional level." President of SCL was Sir Geoffrey Pattie, a former Conservative MP and Defense Minister in Margaret Thatcher's government. SCL's links to the Conservative party extended to the company's chairman, venture capitalist Julian Wheatland. Wheatland also chaired the Oxfordshire Conservatives Association. SCL benefitted from funding by Jonathan Marland, a former Conservative Party Treasurer, trade envoy under David Cameron, and friend of Tory election strategist Lynton Crosby. Property tycoon and Conservative party donor Vincent Tchenguiz was the single largest SCL shareholder for a decade. Another director, Gavin McNicoll, founded the counter-terrorism Eden Intelligence firm which ran a G8 Plus meeting on Financial Intelligence Cooperation at the behest of the British government. Previous board members included Sir James Allen Mitchell, former Prime Minister of the one-time British colony St. Vincent and the Grenadines. Mitchell served as privy counselor to the Queen's advisory board since 1985. Another SCL director was Rear Admiral John Tolhurst, a former assistant director of naval warfare in the Ministry of Defence and *aide de camp* to the Queen. The Queen's third cousin, Lord Ivar Mountbatten, was also on SCL's advisory board but it was unclear if he still held that role at the beginning of 2018.

SCL emerged from murky alliances between venture capitalists and former British military and intelligence officers who were also closely tied to the higher echelons of the Conservative party. The key characters in election meddling were not Russian, Ahmed (2018) concluded: they were British, Eton educated, headquartered in the city of London, and had close ties to Her Majesty's government.

SCL was contracted by the Ministry of Defense for Target Audience Analysis shortly before the 2016 presidential elections, specifically for fiscal year 2014/2015. SCL claimed to have conducted "behavioral change programs" in over 60 countries for clients that included the British Ministry of Defense, the US State Department, and NATO. In May 2015, SCL Defense, another subsidiary, received $1 million (CAD) to support NATO operations in Eastern Europe targeting Russia. The company delivered a three-month course in Riga which taught "advanced counter-propaganda techniques designed to help member states assess and counter Russia's propaganda in Eastern Europe" (O'Hare 2018). NATO's website said the "revolutionary" training would "help Ukrainians better defend themselves against the Russian threat." Such activities placed SCL in a category not altogether distant from "regime change" and "color revolution" tactics that had been evolving, particularly in western hands, at least since the time of the break-up of Yugoslavia.

SCL's website indicated links to the post-coup regime in Kiev. The company took pride in its attempts to support Ukraine's "radical nationalist" regime in its conflict with the breakaway regimes of the Donbass. SCL worked with Kiev and with the British Ministry of Defense in a campaign of information warfare designed to incite sedition in the Donetsk People's Republic and prepare an as yet unfulfilled takeover (Garrie 2018). Promotion of radical nationalism in Ukraine appeared to date back to the so-called Orange Revolution in 2004.

In Argentina, SCL helped securing the election of right-wing candidate Mauricio Macri in the 2015 elections against the then incumbent, "leftist" president Cristina Fernández de Kirchner and her party's candidate to succeed her, Daniel Scioli (House of Commons 2018).

Cambridge Analytica has been described as a shell within SCL, whose cast of characters included (among those close to Donald Trump): Steve Bannon, Andrew Breitbart (who died in 2012 but whose *Breitbart News* was chaired by Steve Bannon), and the billionaire father and daughter team of Robert and Rebekah Mercer. Those involved in devising the Analytica business model included Christopher Wylie, Michael Kosinski, and Alexandre Kogan (Bump 2018). CEO Aleksandr Nix proved an unwitting source of damaging information when he was filmed in a covert 2018 Channel 4 television investigation. This pictured Nix talking about Analytica operations to journalists posing as potential clients (Channel 4 2018). Wikileaks founder Julian Assange became involved when Analytica reportedly suggested working with him to help in the process of publication of hacked (or leaked) DNC emails (Assange declined)(Prokop 2018a).

The method of psycho-profiling devised by Wylie, Kogan, and others is said to have impacted the Leave Campaign for Brexit in the UK in 2016 (Cadwalladr 2018). Analytica was being sued among other things for illegal work it is alleged to have undertaken about that campaign. Special

Counsel Robert Mueller was also looking into links between Analytica and the Trump campaign, probably extending to discussions between Robert Smith, Michael Flynn, and Analytica which among other things touched on the DNC emails. Christopher Wylie (Canadian) contended that the idea for Analytica was something he developed while a student working on his PhD in London. He was recruited by SCL and introduced to Steve Bannon. Bannon liked his ideas: for Bannon, Wylie explained, politics was downstream from culture – to change politics, you changed the culture. Robert Mercer, who had invested up to $1.5 million for a pilot project in the gubernatorial race in Virginia in November 2013 was later to invest $12m in Analytica (Cadwalladr 2018).

Michael Kosinski and David Stillwell (psychology professors at Cambridge University's Psychometrics Center) developed a methodology for integrating Facebook and Twitter "Likes" with OCEAN scores (based on measures of openness to experience, conscientiousness, extraversion, agreeableness, and neuroticism) and data such as TV preferences, airline travel, shopping habits, church attendance, book purchases, and magazine subscriptions (Grassegger and Krogerus 2017). On this basis clients could target individual voters with emotionally charged content. Facebook users were invited to undertake a personality test and in return they were asked to allow the researchers access to the users' profiles (40% consented). At that time (and up until 2015), this also gave researchers access to the accounts of the friends of those who had consented.

Kosinski and Stillwell reported that they had attracted a lot of interest from intelligence agencies, even that there existed third party companies who funded such research on behalf of intelligence agencies. Kosinski claimed that, by using personality targeting, Facebook posts could attract up to 63% more clicks and 1,400 more conversations. This kind of propaganda tracked what people did rather than what they said.

Analytica might have contracted with Kosinski and Stillwell had these wanted less money. Instead, another Cambridge psychologist, Alexsandr Kogan, offered to build an application for harvesting Facebook data that would achieve a comparable outcome more inexpensively. Kogan's company, Global Science Research (GSR), provided the data to Analytica in 2014 in return for $7m (Cadwalladr 2018). The quiz that Kogan offered to Facebook users in order to generate personality data was called *thisisyourdigitallife*. Kogan told Facebook it was for academic research. The ultimate purpose was to match personality and Facebook profile data to voter rolls. Facebook maintained early in 2018 that Analytica still had at least some of the Kogan data. Analytica has variously claimed it did not have the data, or that the data was destroyed two years previously.

Alexsandr Kogan had also worked as associate professor for St. Petersburg University, where his research was funded by the Russian government to analyze "stress, health and psychological wellbeing in social networks" (Cadwalladr and Graham-Harrison 2018). The revelation of Kogan's St Petersburg connection emerged just as relations between Moscow and the west plumbed new lows in the midst of the Skripal scandal. Kogan, a US citizen, was born in the former-Soviet republic of Moldova but moved to the USA as a child. Cambridge University confirmed that Kogan had correctly sought the permission of the head of his Cambridge psychology department to work with St Petersburg: "It was understood that this work and any associated grants would be in a private capacity, separate to his work at the university" (Pinchuk and Busvine 2018). Kogan advised a team at St Petersburg State University that was exploring whether psychopathy, narcissism and Machiavellianism – dubbed the 'dark triad' by psychologists – were linked to abusive online behavior, according to Yanina Ledovaya, senior lecturer at the Petersburg university's department of psychology (ibid).

Analytica also made a pitch to Lukoil, which wanted to explore links between US voters and consumption. The Analytica work would have been shared with its CEO, former Soviet Oil Minister, Vagit Alekperov. The pitch focused on election disruption techniques. Analytica never actually did work for Lukoil, but the company introduced Lukoil to the idea of linking social media data, micro-targeting, and election manipulation (Cadwalladr and Graham-Harrison 2018).

Analytica was a source of data for the Trump campaign via Brad Parscale, the campaign's digital director – hired by Jared Kushner and slated to lead Trump's re-election campaign in 2020. After the demise of Cambridge Analytica in 2018, AP disclosed that four former Analytica employees were working for a company called Data Propria, in whose parent company (Cloud Commerce), Parscale had a substantial ownership interest. Data Propria had a role in 2018 polling-related work for the Republican National Campaign and there was speculation concerning 2020 [Horvitz 2018]). For the Trump campaign, Analytica had 13 people working under Parscale. The campaign's fee to Analytica was $5.9m, of which $5m went towards buying TV ads. But Analytica's head of digital managed an advertising budget of $12m on behalf of Parscale's firm Giles and Parscale – a small slice of the $94m Giles-Parscale was paid to purchase the campaign's ads (Illing 2018).

Special Counsel Robert Mueller requested in 2017 that Cambridge Analytica provide internal documents as part of his investigation into possible collusion between the Trump campaign and Russia during the 2016 election. Trump Campaign insider Michael Flynn had a brief advisory role with Analytica. *Vox.com* asked whether Flynn had been in conversation with

Peter Smith (a pro-Trump GOP operative) as to the possibility of accessing Hillary Clinton's private server's 30,000 deleted emails (Prokop 2017). A *Wall Street Journal* reporter (Harris 2017) had inquired whether Analytica's campaign assistance to Trump helped guide Russia's voter targeting scheme. Campaign executive director Michael Glassner has said that the Republican National Committee was the Trump campaign's primary source of voter data. Parscale claimed that Analytica provided only analysis, not raw data (Illing 2018). Parscale also denied that the campaign had utilized psychographic targeting.

What did Analytica provide then? It provided a daily tracker of voting, "persuasion online media buying," identified which potential voters in the RNC files were most likely to be persuadable (undecided but swinging towards Trump), and created a visualization tool that showed in each state which areas were most persuadable, and what those voters cared about (a heat map of the country to pinpoint where Trump should visit to maximize his impact on potentially persuadable voters; Lapowsky 2017). Other sources show that Analytica conducted hundreds of thousands of voter surveys for the Trump Campaign to better understand the Trump voter. RNC and the Trump campaign ran 175,000 variations of the same ad on Facebook on the day of the third presidential debate in October 2016 (ibid).

Brittany Kaiser's evidence and that of Channel 4 Television investigations go further, referring to the invention by Analytica of the "crooked Hillary" moniker, the establishment of a Defeat Crooked Hillary super Pac, and the micro-targeting of religious and other communities. Managing director of the political division, Mark Turnball, was recorded as saying "we did all the research, all the analytics, all the targeting, the television campaign, and our data informed all the strategy . . . (pushing this) onto millions of social media users" in ways that were not branded, attributable, or traceable (cited in Hilder 2019). Chief data officer Alex Tayler was quoted as saying "You did your rallies in the right locations, you moved more people out in those key swing states on election day. That's how we won the election" (ibid).

How effective was Analytica?

Samuel Woolley, head of Computational Propaganda Project at Oxford Internet Institute, concluded that a "disproportionate amount of pro-Trump messaging was spread via automated bots and anti-Hillary propaganda. Trump's bots outnumbered Clinton's by 5 to 1." Woolley claimed that 1,000 or more bots can potentially change the algorithm of a site. Bots can react instantly to trending topics, producing targeted posts, images, even YouTube videos, and can capture what people are thinking at a particular moment and then serve it back to them, over and over again (Illing 2018).

But it is not known that any Analytica data ever got to the Russians, nor even how useful Analytica was to the Trump campaign.

Martin Moore (head of Center for the Study of Media, Communication and Power at King's College) told the *Guardian*'s Carol Cadwalladr (2018) that Trump's campaign was "using 40,000–50,000 variants of ads every day that were continuously measuring responses and then adopting and evolving based on that response." Analytica was able to use this real-time information to determine which messages were resonating and where, and then to shape Trump's travel schedule around it.

Alexander Nix and/or other Cambridge Analytica senior executives, as revealed by Channel 4 Television investigations and in evidence and recordings made available by whistleblower Brittany Kaiser, indicate that Analytica used psychographics to help elevate Ted Cruz to second-most threatening contender in the primaries (Timmons 2018). Facebook was aware of this but took no action other than a letter. John Bolton (Trump's national security adviser, appointed in 2018) had earlier established a super PAC which, according to the *New York Times*, had contracted with Analytica in August 2014 (Rosenberg 2018). It hired Analytica to develop psychological profiles of voters, using data harvested from tens of millions of Facebook profiles, according to former Analytica employees and company documents. Bolton's PAC spent $1.2m for survey research over two years (and $5 million between 2014 and 2017). The service included behavioral micro-targeting with psychographic messaging. For example, the Bolton campaign wanted to make people more militaristic in their worldview. The PAC also supported Thom Tillis, GOP senator from North Carolina. SCL wanted to use the voter contact lists available to Bolton's campaign to direct people "toward the Facebook application." Later, Analytica wrote up talking points for Bolton (O'Sullivan and Griffin 2018a). Thus Analytica played a significant role for super PACs in the 2014 mid-term elections (in the form of polling, focus groups, and message development; Rosenberg et al 2018).

Channel 4 Television investigations and recordings released by Brittany Kaiser (for the documentary *The Great Hack* [Amer and Noujaim 2019] and in interview with Paul Hilder [2019]) include references by Alexander Nix to various international operations of Analytica or its parent SCL. These included bribing opposition leaders, facilitating election-stealing, and suppressing voter turnout – for example, by encouraging voter apathy, promoting cynicism, and organizing anti-election rallies on the day of polling in opposition strongholds – and generally engaging in election black ops (Nix denies such allegations). In Kenya, Analytica worked to raise support for President Kenyatta's Jubilee party, conducting surveys of hopes (jobs) and fears (tribal violence) and employing divisive propaganda and disinformation. Its influence spread from surveys to legacy media (Channel 4, 2018).

In Nigeria, ahead of the 2015 elections, a Nigerian billionaire paid Analytica $2m to hack into the medical records of General Muhummadu Buhari, then candidate of the All Progressives Congress. Incumbent President Johnathan did not necessarily know of this. Israeli cybersecurity contractors were involved – they provided the hacked documents and Analytica had the responsibility of finding incriminating materials. Critics have observed that Analytica did not seem too concerned about the security of its own employees in Lagos (Kazeem 2018). In Yemen, Cambridge Analytica's parent company SCL launched Project Titania in 2009 in areas of Yemen's Marib province and al-Mukalla city in Hadramaut province. Working on behalf of a US-based military contractor, SCL's role was to reduce what it identified as "non-desired behaviors" or NDBs (Nord 2018).

Factors that mitigate against the presumption that Analytica – whether or not it acted within the law – actually wielded the huge influence of which it boasted to clients include the following considerations:

- Methodological issues having to do with the limitations of social psychology as a predictive science and tests of significance need to be weighed.
- Limitations of multi-variate analysis, in which some variables have only a very loose connection to actual political issues or candidates.
- The relative unpredictability of the impact of human self-reflection and the tendency on the part of positivist researchers to underestimate intelligence and learning.
- The operation of standard processes of selective exposure, attention, and retention, which tend to limit the impact of new messages in favor of existing beliefs, attitudes and behaviors.
- Finally, the problem of how to evaluate this kind of influence when compared with that of powerful legacy media (e.g. Fox Television) and with classic lobbying. Was the "Crooked Hillary" moniker successful because of its pervasiveness throughout legacy media, or social media, or both?

(ABC News 2018)

Classic lobbying tactics might include the influence of fixers such as Tom Barrack (Kirkpatrick 2018), Elliot Broidy (Waldman 2018), George Nader (Aleem 2018), and their purported relationships to figures such as Donald Trump, Jared Kushner, and Steve Bannon. Such links figured in the remit for special counsel Robert Mueller. Barrack was a wealthy Lebanese American supporter of Trump who acted as a go-between of sorts between UAE and Trump Campaign interests. Nader was a Lebanese businessman and go-between for the Abu Dhabi crown prince. Broidy was a Jewish-American businessman with vast UAE and Israeli interests and close to Israeli premier, Benjamin Netanyahu. This may relate to Saudi/UAE pressure in 2017 on Qatar, and to money flows from multiple countries to Washington.

More importantly, the Cambridge Analytica scandal has alerted the public to a broader industry specializing in the exploitation of big data and depending in significant measure on social media for commercial, promotional, and political purposes. Was Russia a significant player in this industry? Probably not.

Trump/Analytica was not the first

Statements by former President Obama's director of integration and media for his 2012 campaign, Carol Davidsen, indicated that Facebook had discovered but tolerated the Obama campaign's massive data-mining operation. This involved one million supporters who gave the campaign permission to look at their Facebook friend lists. The campaign, which "sucked up the whole social graph" was allowed because Facebook was "on Obama's side" (Investor's Business Daily, 2018).

Then there was i360 Themis. Investigative reporter Greg Palast claimed that this company, an operation he linked to the Koch brothers, pioneered the art of dynamic psychometric manipulation and tracked 1,800 behaviors including credit card purchase, cable TV choices etc. Its competitor was DataTrust founded by Karl Rove (deputy chief of staff to the George W. Bush administration) and funded by hedge fund manager Paul Singer. There were comparable companies offering database matching of names for the purpose of purging voter rolls, in Florida and elsewhere. "RapLeaf" in 2010 was collecting and reselling data it had gathered from third party Facebook applications to marketing firms and political consultants. Facebook cut off RapLeaf's data access (Palast 2018). Speaking on behalf of an Oxford University study in 2018, Samantha Bradshaw indicated that the Cambridge Analytica model was lucrative and widespread:

> It's really hard to say exactly how much money each campaign has been spending. When we released our report recently that kind of looked at this phenomenon more globally, we had about 48 countries, and dating back until about 2010. From publicly available information, we found half a billion dollars being spent by governments and political parties on these kinds of strategies. So there's definitely big business behind it. But putting a solid number, it's still very hard to do.
> (Bradshaw in interview with Sharmini Peries on
> Real News Network 2018)

Placed in broader context, allegations of Russian uses of social media for the purposes of "meddling" in the 2016 elections, even if taken at face value, appear neither new nor sophisticated. That is a principal lesson offered by Cambridge Analytica. A further lesson is that the efficacy of such techniques has been exaggerated especially when the influence of mainstream legacy media, lobbying (overt or otherwise), and the broader informational environment are factored in. Notwithstanding their actual (in)efficacy, there is no shortage of interest in experimenting, as demonstrated by numerous western players, some of whom appear close to the world of intelligence.

5   Implications for social media

What are the implications of RussiaGate for social media?

Facebook's $40bn advertising business (accounting for 98% of revenue [Statista 2018]) is built on user willingness to volunteer personal information. Given Facebook's claim to two billion users, the value of such data was unrivalled. Facebook encouraged broad or "big data" collection. It made sense to motivate developers to build applications on top of its platform. API was the feature allowing program developers to interface with Facebook. "Permissiveness is a feature, as they say, not a bug" (Roose 2018). Even after 2015 Facebook allowed some companies, including four giant Chinese enterprises, special access to data and, in some cases, data about users' friends (Laforgia and Dance 2018; Seetharaman 2018).

Writing for AP, Barbara Ortutay (2018) noted that Facebook could provide users with all the data it possessed about them, including data that determined which ads to show and which posts to emphasize. But few users bothered to read Facebook's privacy policy. Additionally, Facebook offered a set of controls allowing users to limit how their information would be used. Users could turn off ad targeting and see only generic ads. But they would first need to go into the ad settings and uncheck all their interests, interactions with companies and websites. Facebook put users in target categories based on their activity. It could even keep the typing keystrokes that a user had started and then deleted. Increasingly, Facebook tried to match what it knew about a user with offline data that it purchased from data brokers or gathered in other ways. It could draw inferences about a user that the user had no intention of sharing. These types of data collection were not necessarily explicit in privacy policies or settings. Advertisers were not given access to the raw data. They merely informed Facebook what kind of people they wanted their ads to reach; Facebook would make the matches and show the data. Applications also collected a lot of data about users.

In the wake of RussiaGate and Cambridge Analytica scandals, Facebook promised to introduce important changes (Kharpal 2018). It would clearly label political ads and require anyone who wanted to run ads that related to political campaigns, civil rights, immigration, guns, economy, and other issues, to prove they were in the USA by supplying the last four digits of their social security number together with a picture of a government-issued ID. Facebook announced plans to hire up to 4,000 more people to review and verify political ads. Their role would likely include navigating the nuance of what was and wasn't "political."

It may be argued that social media were culpable for the extent to which their networks had been abused for propaganda and related purposes. Social media have contributed in no small measure to the relative decline of legacy media, including the advertising models that underwrote them (Auletta 2018). Social media contributed to the uncertainties and confusion concomitant with a "post-truth" era. Yet they were also often seen by politicians as potential saviors, as self-regulators or co-regulators, indispensable contributors to political efforts to (1) boost the autonomy of social media users as information consumers; (2) enhance the transparency, dependability, and legality of social media content; and (3) foreground strongly credible sources.

The European Union sought to impose more "self-censorship" by Google and Facebook, requiring the companies to create programs – answerable to nobody, critics objected – to trawl and delete content (EU 2018). By 2018, Facebook employed well in excess of 10,000 censors working to this purpose in centers in Berlin, Barcelona, and elsewhere. Between Jan–June 2017, according to Facebook, some 75% of 300,000 deleted accounts were taken out before their first tweet. As soon as it became aware of a piece of "terrorist" content, Facebook claimed, it would remove 83% of subsequently uploaded copies within one hour of upload (Ike 2018). The EU advocated stronger measures regarding terrorism, incitement, child sexual abuse, counterfeit products, and copyright infringement.

The scandals of "RussiaGate" and "Cambridge Analytica," while negative on the face of it for the social media companies, seem also to be strengthening public perceptions of their relative power and importance, perceptions that in turn cede them even more power, influence, and control over the public's information environment than they had previously employed. For example:

1   The Mexican government negotiated with social media giants Facebook, Google and Twitter ahead of the July 2018 elections to award these media potential scope to influence the behavior of electors through information about polling dates, reminders to vote, disclosures of times

of voting, directions to polling stations, and news about the progress of elections. The Mexican electoral authority INE agreed to provide Facebook with real-time data on election night and provide physical space in INE where Facebook could perform election-related activities. Critics feared that the companies' abilities to use algorithms to censor search results and reduce the impact of posts were ripe for electoral manipulation (Gonzalez and Lobo 2018a). Such fears were allayed to some extent by the resounding electoral victory of anti-establishment candidate Andrés Manuel López Obrador.

2   Early in 2018, Facebook announced plans to reduce "political" posts from newsfeeds (Isaac 2018).

3   The potential for political censorship was illustrated by Facebook's decision in May 2018 to shut down the Arizona Educators Rank and File Committee pages, whose purpose was to provide a forum for teachers in Arizona and other states to communicate and oppose what they considered to be the betrayal of their struggles by unions (White 2018). In another case, in September 2018, Facebook announced that it had removed 652 accounts which it claimed were promoting anti-Saudi, anti-Israel, and pro-Palestinian themes. Twitter deleted nearly 300 such accounts while Google and YouTube also deleted at least one. A cybersecurity firm called FireEye run by a former US Air Force officer with a background in cyber espionage had tipped off Facebook, Twitter, and Google to the alleged accounts (Nord 2018b).

4   Facebook and Google decided, as discussed in Spring (2018), to stop "domain fronting," an anti-censorship application that disguised traffic to make it look like traffic from others' websites. This enabled users to hide behind or within these other websites in order to avoid censorship, but could be faulted for its inherent lack of transparency.

5   Since at least summer 2017, social media adopted algorithms whose results appeared to be biased against alternative news sites and in favor of mainstream, middle-of-the-road websites. This worked to the disadvantage of sites that were associated with more left-wing or more right-wing positions. This measure had little or nothing to do with the *quality* of information and everything to do with control over dissident *analysis* and *opinion*. Many alternative sites (e.g. the *World Socialist Website*) reported a sharp falloff in numbers of visitors directed to their daily news stories from other sites. In many cases this had negatively impacted the business models that underwrite such sites (Damon and Niemuth 2017).

By 2018 many noted independent news websites had shut down as a result of such restrictions. Those that remained considered they were being censored like never before, with social media traffic from Facebook and Twitter completely cut off in some cases (Webb 2018b). A special survey by *MintPress* in August 2017 reported a Google algorithm targeting "fake news" that quashed traffic to many independent news and advocacy sites, such as the *American Civil Liberties Union, Democracy Now!*, and *WikiLeaks*. These experienced massive drops in flows of news to their sites as a result of searches. The *World Socialist Website* reported a 67% decrease in Google search returns; *MintPress* reported a decrease of 76% (Webb 2017b) and average traffic to its page fell from 70,000 unique visitors in January 2018 to 4,000 and even zero by June. In other cases, traffic had fallen close to zero. *Antimedia*, with over two million likes and followers, saw traffic drop from 300,000 to 12,000 page views per day in the space of a year. Some pages promoting natural health news along with political content saw their pages deleted without warning by Facebook. *Collectively Conscious*, with over 900,000 likes and follows, was deleted without warning after Facebook said the page "violated its terms of use agreement" but did not state which terms had been violated. *Nikola Tesla, Earth We Are One*, and similar pages were likewise suddenly deleted without explanation. In August 2018, Facebook summarily deleted several pages of Alex Jones (of *Infowars* notoriety) and in the same month Google's YouTube suspended the Alex Jones channel – with 2.4 million subscribers. Facebook suspended 87 accounts linked to the Brazilian far-right *Movimento Brasil Livre* (MBL – Free Brazil Movement) organization; and Facebook-owned WhatsApp messaging app announced that, worldwide, it would cut the maximum number of recipients for forwarded messages from 250 to 20. Facebook took down the page of Venezuela-headquartered international television news agency *teleSUR* for the second time in a year without any specific reason being provided. Facebook also shut down accounts that it claimed were "bad actors" in an influence campaign targeting the 2018 mid-term elections which might have been linked to Russia, although no actual evidence of such links was supplied. The pages had spent a combined $11,000 on 150 ads and had been "careful to cover their tracks"; yet most of the "bad actor" pages and accounts had hardly any followers, with most of them having *no* followers. The main event cited by Facebook (which deleted the page linked to it), the *No Unite the Right 2 – DC* rally, had been organized months before the page alleged to be behind it had been created.

The "bad actor" pages were identified with help from the Atlantic Council's Digital Forensic Research Lab (DFRLab). The team of four individuals running the DFR Lab was headed by a former National Security Council employee, Graham Brookie, who was also its founder. Facebook officially partnered with the Atlantic Council, a "think tank" (or pro-NATO agency) in May 2018 to tackle so-called fake news, claiming that the Atlantic Council would serve as its "eyes and ears" in identifying alleged foreign-influence operations (Webb 2018c).

Durden cited a Reuters report that Facebook had by this time become a top donor to Atlantic Council (Durden 2018d), alongside the British government. By its own admission, the initial hostile target of Atlantic Council was "the left of the political spectrum" which it charged with seeking "to promote divisions and set Americans against one another." Of the removal of the *No Unite the Right 2* page, one critic observed that

> as part of a campaign to block what it called "divisive," "violent," and "extremist" activity, Facebook, working in conjunction with US intelligence agencies, announced Tuesday that it had blocked not the Nazi rally, but an event page for the demonstration protesting it.
>
> (Damon 2018d)

In September 2018, Facebook announced that it had purged more than 800 US publishers and accounts for politically oriented content that violated the company's spam policies. The accounts and pages were probably domestic actors using clickbait headlines and similar tactics to drive users to websites where they could be targeted with ads. Some had hundreds of thousands of followers and expressed a range of political viewpoints (Dwoskin and Romm 2018a, b). Some of the media outlets removed had previously been targeted in a ("PropOrnot") anonymous blacklist of oppositional sites published by the *Washington Post* in November 2016. They included *Anti-Media*, with 2.1 million followers, *Free Thought Project*, with 3.1 million followers, and *Counter Current News*, with 500,000 followers (Damon 2018b).

Just prior to the mid-term US elections in 2018, Facebook announced the shutdown of 115 social media accounts on its Facebook and Instagram platforms upon being advised by US law enforcement about online activity that was thought to be linked to foreign entities. Action was taken before investigations were complete. In response to representation from *Democracy Party* sources Twitter deleted 10,000 "automated accounts" in September and October that appeared to be from Democrats yet "discouraged people from voting on election day." A few weeks earlier Facebook had removed 82 pages, accounts and groups which it claimed had originated in Iran. Writing for the *World Socialist Web Site*, Kevin Reed (2018) claimed that these measures targeted specifically left-wing and oppositional content on Facebook critical of government policies in the USA and the UK. A leaked Google memo from this period indicated that Silicon Valley giants were now beginning to prefer the value of "civility" over that of freedom of speech.

In an October statement co-authored by Facebook Head of Cybersecurity, Nathaniel Gleicher, Facebook announced that it had removed 559 pages and 251 accounts "that have consistently broken our rules against spam and coordinated inauthentic behavior," i.e. "sensational" political content – regardless of its political slant – to build an audience and drive traffic to their websites. In other words, Caitlin Johnstone (2018a, c) observed, pages were removed for publishing controversial political content and trying to get people to read it.

The following month Facebook claimed that between April and September 2018 it had found and removed "roughly 1.5 billion fake accounts, while targeting 12.4 million pieces of terrorist propaganda, 2.2 billion pieces of spam and 66 million pieces of content that ran afoul of rules barring adult nudity and sexual activity" (Dwoskin and Romm 2018b). The company promised to create an independent board to review people's appeals of Facebook's decisions, and publish the minutes of its meetings whenever new content policies were decided.

6   Systems of supposed "verification" run by social media in collaboration with established mainstream media are problematic. For example, Facebook, Google, and Twitter participated in #Verified2018, a project that brought together major national and international media outlets to unilaterally dictate what they deemed to be "verified" information, and seeking to present oppositional sources as "fake news." The campaign was spearheaded by *Animal Politics*, a supposedly independent news site that was actually funded by the Ford Foundation and the Open Society Foundation, and enjoyed close ties to US intelligence (Gonzalez and Lobo 2018b). Some pages flagged – not always accurately – as "fake news" by Facebook "fact checking" partner organizations, like the Associated Press and Snopes (Leetaru 2016), and pages that share such stories, are punished by Facebook. *The Mind Unleashed* – with 8.8 million likes and follows – was warned and threatened for just such an "offense" (Webb 2018b, c).

7   As already noted, Facebook has partnered with the Atlantic Council (a pro-NATO "think tank") from May 2018 for the purpose of monitoring "for misinformation and foreign interference." Atlantic Council's Digital Forensic Research Lab said that the goal was to design tools "to bring us closer together" instead of "driving us further apart." FAIR responded:

> Much like "counter-espionage" is another name for espionage, "counter-propaganda" efforts are just propaganda efforts. How exactly will the Atlantic Council define "misinformation" and "disinformation," and what "foreign interference" will merit the highest priority?
>
> (Johnson 2018)

8   Social media perform significant work for the security establishment. This poisons their capacity for independence and transparency. For example:

(a)   Amazon, Microsoft, and Google competed to secure a multi-billion-dollar Department of Defense contract to build and oversee the US military's Cloud computing infrastructure, which would be used to control every aspect of the Pentagon's global operations (Morrow 2018a). Employees at Microsoft and Google have tried to resist such contracting. Amazon CEO Jeff Bezos announced in October that his company would continue to accept Pentagon contracts (it already had contracted with the CIA) that included work on a $10 billion cloud-computing project. In 2014 a $600 million computing cloud project developed by Amazon Web Services for the CIA began servicing all 17 agencies that make up the intelligence community (Konkel 2014). A long-term prize for Amazon would be selection as the military's sole procurement source for off-the-shelf components (Ditz 2018c).

(b)   In 2017 Google won a share of the contract for the Defense Department's Maven program, which uses artificial intelligence to interpret video images and can improve the targeting of drone strikes. In response to protests from the company's own employees, this program was scaled back to avoid involvement in lethal activity (Shane and Wakabayashi 2018).

(c)   The CIA publishes press releases on all the social media ventures it sponsors, via its technology investment arm In-Q-Tel. Google partnered with the CIA from 2004 when the company bought Keyhole, a mapping technology business that eventually became Google Earth. In 2010, Google and In-Q-Tel made a joint investment in a company called Recorded Future, whose goal was a "temporal analytics engine" that scours the web and creates curves that predict where events may head (Edwards 2011).

(d)   WikiLeaks founder Julian Assange has described Facebook as the "most appalling spy machine" ever invented. Users are creating the "world's most comprehensive database" for US Intelligence (Brian 2011).

As in so many other dimensions, consideration of the role of social media (but not only of *social* media) and RussiaGate leads back to the intelligence agencies, and this will be focus of the next chapter.

6 Fake news and intelligence

Enter "spooks"

There has always been a close relationship between instances of "fake news" and the operations of intelligence services and other propagandists working on behalf of state power. Much of this falls into the category of deflective source propaganda (Jowett and O'Donnell 2014). I have previously referenced some examples. These included the work of William Stephenson, a British spy charged by Churchill to persuade America to join Britain in World War II in the wake of the Dunkirk disaster of 1940. Stephenson's massive MI6 operation incorporated a news agency and a New Jersey–based radio station that would air disinformation fed to it from other operatives (Simkin 2014). In another early example, the founder of public relations, Edward Bernays, in conjunction with the White House under Eisenhower and with the CIA (led by Alan Dulles) orchestrated the overthrow of democratically elected Jacobo Arbenz of Guatemala in 1953. Bernays's "deflecting-awareness-of-the-source" propaganda encompassed the setting up of a Central America news agency that carried false news about the Arbenz regime. This in turn was picked up and distributed by Western media (Tye 2002; Chapman 2009). In the run up to the 1990 election in Nicaragua the CIA planted false stories in German newspapers about how Sandanista leaders, then the incumbent revolutionary power, held Swiss bank accounts (for more such stories, see Davies 2009). The Washington candidate, Violeta Chamarro, won.

More recent instances have been afforded by the Syrian Observatory of Human Rights in Syria (SOAR) and the White Helmets. These were funded by multiple Western governments (UK Foreign Office, USAID, Holland, Germany) throughout much of the so-called Syrian civil war from 2011 to 2018, operating principally from jihadist-controlled territories that were dangerous for western correspondents to report from, and were often the sole source of news and propaganda, picked up and used uncritically by western mainstream media (Cartalucci 2013; Blumenthal 2016; Boyd-Barrett 2019b). The White Helmets were established and largely trained in Turkey following initiation of the force in 2013 by British ex-military officer James Le Mesurier, whose business was establishing "stabilization" programs in conflict zones, with the benefit of seed funding from Japan, the UK, and the USA (Beeley 2018; Hayward 2017; Webb 2017). They were intended in part to help rebuild communities after conflict but also operated as mechanisms for the infiltration of "post-conflict communities" on behalf of sponsoring western nations. Le Mesurier has conceded that "it is unrealistic to expect the (Syrian Civil Defense) SCD members, the majority of whom come from majority Sunni communities, to remain neutral on a personal level. A perpetual problem with these programs is the failure to be inclusive, as seen in failed demobilization efforts in Libya" (Speakman 2015).

Bellingcat.com, sometimes celebrated as a shoestring, citizen-based online initiative but linked to the pro-NATO Atlantic Council, and focusing solely on matters of interest to NATO from a NATO-friendly perspective, fed controversial social media–based claims to influence mainstream media framing against the Assad regime throughout various instances of the alleged use of chemical weapons, and to influence media framing against Russia in the 2014 MH17 controversy (Boyd-Barrett 2018; Boyd-Barrett 2017). Bellingcat's founder Eliot Higgins was reported in 2018 to have promoted an online account, *ShamiWitness* that supported and recruited on behalf of ISIS. The account was run by a 24-year-old Indian marketing executive Mehdi Biswas, based in Bangalore, who had little to no Middle East expertise. Although deleted in 2014 after a Channel 4 exposure, *Shami-Witness* was regarded as a meaningful source of ISIS-related information by many mainstream western media (Webb 2018d).

Intelligence activity in the Trump-era of fake news

In earlier chapters I have examined the Steele Dossier and the Intelligence Community Assessment of January 2017 as significant conduits of intelligence community intervention into RussiaGate. In this section I shall turn to the Skripal affair of 2018, leaving consideration of the hacking/leaking controversies surrounding 2016 publication of the DNC emails to the next chapter.

The Skripal affair

The Skripal case is linked to RussiaGate both indirectly (as yet another manifestation of managed western anti-Russian hysteria contributing to RussiaGate propaganda in the USA) and directly (overlap of *dramatis personae*). The leak from the Anonymous hacking group in January 2019 of "Integrity Initiative" documents (see Introduction) suggested that the

British handling of its relations with Russia in the Skripal affair might have been scripted in advance. The Institute of Statecraft had planned a detailed anti-Russian propaganda war, including "potential levers" to bring about Russian "behavior change" (Stevens 2019).

As a case-study of contemporary propaganda, the Skripal narrative has at least two major chapters, of which I have space here only for the first. This has to do with the attempted assassination of Sergei Skripal and his daughter Yulia in March 2018 and British government claims of Russian culpability. The second chapter, which I deal with elsewhere (see Boyd-Barrett 2019a), concerns the accidental death some months later of Dawn Sturgess, and British government claims to have identified members of a Russian assassination team responsible for the poisoning of both the Skripals and of Dawn Sturgess and her partner.

Christopher Steele may have been linked indirectly to the Skripal case (the poisoning of Sergei and Yulia Skripal on March 4, 2018 in Salisbury, UK). Skripal, working for Russian military intelligence (GRU), was recruited as a double agent to MI6 in the early 1990s by Pablo Miller, then based in Estonia at the time that Steele was working undercover for MI6 in Moscow (Mendick et al 2018). Steele, when recalled home to take over the Russia desk in London from 2006 to 2009, would likely have had access to reports submitted by Skripal prior to his arrest in Russia in 2004 (he was released in a spy-swap in 2010; O'Neill 2018). Miller had worked for Steele and Steele's company Orbis, and there has been speculation as to whether Skripal was also a source for the Steele dossier (e.g. see West 2018).

It is not possible at the time of writing to dismiss Russia as a potential culprit for the attempted assassination of Skripal and his daughter, but equally it has not been possible to assert such a claim in an evidence-based fashion beyond reasonable doubt. Theoretically, the job of the press is to stay open to reasonable doubt and to be duly skeptical of "authoritative" claims. In this case (not uncharacteristically) the mainstream press (with some exceptions) manifestly failed.

The main points to consider in assessing the official narrative of what happened in Salisbury in the spring of 2018 are these:

1   Identification of the nerve agent novichok (A-234) or rather, a novichoks-*type* agent (important distinction) – said to be a much more potent Russian version of the British-American VX – was disclosed by Porton Down's Gary Aitkenhead, chief executive of the government's Defence Science and Technology Laboratory (DSTL) on April 2 (Morris and Crerar 2018). (A much earlier mention, March 8, of the term novichock appeared in a blog post for Bellingcat.com from a writer paid by Integrity Initiative [Klarenberg 2019]).

Aitkenhead could not determine the source of this sample, whether Russia or anywhere else. This was days *after* Prime Minister Theresa May and British foreign secretary Boris Johnson in the period March 12–14 claimed that the nerve agent thought to have been applied was novichok and that it was "overwhelmingly likely" that Russian president Vladimir Putin had personally ordered the attack. Aitkenhead's statement also came several days *after* the UK and US and many allied countries had taken "retaliatory" action against Russia, starting with Britain's announcement of the expulsion of 23 Russian diplomats on March 14. This was followed by similar expulsions over the following two weeks by governments of over 20 countries (Birnbaum 2018).

Speaking in the House of Commons as early as March 6, the British foreign secretary was already implicating Russia. Sushi (2018) notes that the Salisbury hospital that treated the victims went into lockdown at 11:00 on the morning of March 5. As this likely represents the time of first awareness that the poison in question was from some source other than Fentanyl (an initial suspect), there was insufficient time between March 5 and March 6 for Porton Down to have prepared the blood samples necessary for identification of the metabolites – structure of a poison after it has passed through a human body – of a substance supposedly not well understood even as late as September 2015. Yet by the following day, March 7, police sources announced that the Skripals had been "poisoned by a nerve agent in a targeted murder attempt" (ibid).

The principal body authorized for an assessment of a chemical in such circumstances was the Organization for the Prohibition of Chemical Weapons (OPCW). The OPCW team did not arrive until March 21, and they took several weeks to compile their report, which appeared on April 12, long after the British government had asserted the source of poison and guilty party. The OPCW determined that the nerve agent was a highly pure sample, making it difficult therefore to pinpoint a trace of its origin. Its purity suggested that it had been assembled in a highly competent laboratory and in a small quantity. This made it unlikely, therefore, to have been "military grade," as the British had insisted, since such a laboratory would have manufactured it in relatively large quantity, yielding greater impurity. It was very unlikely to have been applied to a door handle (Sushi 2018) – the preferred theory of the British government – since it would have been very difficult to prepare a pure variety for such an application. And had it come from Russia it would very unlikely have been correctly identifiable as A-234 by Boris Johnson as early as March 12, since such confidence in judgement would have required a considerable degree of advance research and knowledge, not in Russia but in Britain. The earliest date the OPCW team might have conducted environmental sampling would have been March 21. The eagerness to blame Russia suggested that the British government's interpretation and handling of the entire incident amounted to an opportunistic but premeditated attempt to smear Russia and recklessly exacerbate the gathering escalation of hostile western rhetoric against Russia or at least that the poisoning was seized upon amateurishly for this purpose, before relevant evidence became available.

Even as late as May 1, the Prime Minister's National Security Adviser Sir Mark Sedwill said that there were no suspects in the investigation of the incident, while, on June 5, Deputy Assistant Commissioner of the Metropolitan Police Dean Haydon confirmed that "there are still a number of lines of inquiry being progressed" (UK Russian Embassy 2018).

2   UK claims that the A-234 organophosphate compound novichok could only have come from Russia were patently false. The president of the Czech Republic reported that his country had produced, tested, and destroyed a small quantity as recently as 2017 (AP 2018). In late 2016, Iranian scientists succeeded in synthesizing a number of novichoks, in full cooperation with the OPCW, and they immediately reported the results to the OPCW so that these could be added to the OPCW's chemical weapons database (Murray 2018a). Other countries had also tested novichoks (see McKeigue and Robinson 2018). Whereas some states like Israel and North Korea had not ratified the Chemical Weapons Convention, nor joined the OPCW, nor destroyed chemical weapons stocks, Russia had cooperated in the OPCW destruction of all its chemical weapons stocks, completed in 2017, which process included the regular OPCW inspection of all the sites alleged to have been in the original novichoks program.

In any case, as we have seen, Porton Down's Chief Scientist said that he could not establish where the poison had originated. He did not deny that Britain possessed novichoks, merely asserting that there was no possible way in which such a nerve agent could ever have been taken out of Porton Down (Morris and Crerar 2018). It was highly likely that the USA and the UK would have researched novichoks. The USA was party to the decontamination from 1999 of the chemical weapon facility at which novichoks had been said (by Vil Mirzayanov, head of Soviet technical counterintelligence) to have been manufactured in Uzbekistan (Miller 1999). Mirzayanov had referenced an apparent understanding between the USA and Russia, presumably extended throughout the membership of the OPCW, to keep the existence of novichoks relatively secret and outside the "Annex of Chemicals" of the Chemical Weapons Convention (Knip 2018). Knip's evaluation of the novichok evidence led him to conclude that "there are strong indications that the West has secretly started to synthesize the substances soon after discovery."

3   UK claims that only Russia could have "weaponized" novichoks were equally false. The major insider source for this claim, Vil Mirzayanov, had first revealed the existence of novichoks in 1992. His story was received skeptically by some scientists. After facing Soviet charges – later dropped – he defected to the USA in 1996. Mirzayanov published relevant formulae in his 2008 self-published book *State Secrets: An Insider's Chronicle of the Russian Chemical Weapons Program*. Knip cites credible sources who suggest that Mirzayanov's formulae were correct, although his assertions that the substances were undetectable and their effects incurable had been confounded by the Skripal case. His assertions that the substance had been successfully weaponized are equally open to doubt. Mirzayanov's credibility had been compromised: he led a US-sponsored attempt to establish an independent Tatarstan – a republic of the Russian Federation, whose capital is Kazan – in the 2000s. On October 26, 2008, he was elected to the Presidium of the Milli Mejlis of the Tatar People and "prime minister" of their "government in exile." In other words, Mirzayanov appeared to be an actor in a US-sponsored program of regime-change and had every reason to be hostile to Russia.

While Mirzayanov alleged that only Russia had ever developed novichoks, this was contested not only by recent clear evidence to the contrary, as we have seen, but also by Vladimir Uglev, a Soviet-era scientist involved in the development of nerve agents 1972–1988, who did not rule out the possibility that novichoks had also been developed by Britain or Germany. Whether or not Russia had succeeded in weaponizing novichoks, it claimed to have suspended the program and acceded to the Chemical Weapons Convention in 1997. It was Uglev who revealed that novichok had been used in the case of a 1995 Mafiosi-style killing – the poisoning of banker Ivan Kivelidi and his assistant by an associate of Kivelidi. Leonid Rink, who had headed the Soviet novichok program, confessed that he had supplied the toxin through intermediaries (Serhan and Mahanta 2018).

4   UK claims that Russia was the only country that could have had a motive to attempt the assassination of the Skripals were patently false. In fact, on the face of it, Russia had very little motive. Why would it wish to draw unwelcome international attention to itself at such a delicate time in western-Russian relations, just prior to its hosting of the World Cup in Saint Petersburg? Why would it wish to undermine the

convention by which spies who have been released in spy-exchanges are left in peace – an understanding that provides security for all parties to such swaps? If Russia had wanted to punish Skripal for his past actions, notwithstanding that he had once languished in a Russian prison and could have been dealt with then, why did it wait for eight years to do so?

By contrast, British intelligence may well have had a motive, perhaps relating in some way to mooted collaboration between UK and US intelligence in compilation of the Steele dossier. Additionally, as a double agent whose work might reasonably be supposed to have contributed to the deaths or at least have compromised the security of Soviet/Russian spies when he worked for MI6, Skripal would doubtless have given many enemies sufficient motive to try to kill him, perhaps especially if these enemies had stumbled on any of the novichok samples sold by Leonid Rink to Mafiosi in 1995/1996. US investigative journalist Seymour Hersh lent his support to such reflections with his claim in July 2018 that Skripal had likely been briefing British intelligence on Russian organized crime (RT 2018c). Both Sergei and Yulia Skripal had reportedly switched off their cell phones as they visited parks in Salisbury and Amesbury (also a haunt for Charlie Rowley and Dawn Sturgess who were later to get caught up in the Skripal narrative) on March 4 and earlier that day Sergei had reportedly acted in a very agitated way while father and daughter lunched in a restaurant. Had they taken something that had been spiked with an incapacitating substance, such as fentanyl (Cunningham 2018b, c)? While comatose in a secured hospital wing, the Skripals' blood samples could have been contaminated with novichok.

5   Novichoks were not included in the OPCW list of nerve agents until very recently. Their inclusion had been discussed, but US representatives, under pressure from Hillary Clinton's State Department, discouraged such talk. Knip (2018) cited Wikileaks publications of US diplomatic cables transmitted after the publication of Mirzayanov's 2008 book to the effect that the US embassy in The Hague was instructed to avoid any substantive discussion about the book and to "discourage that discussion and report all cases in which the book is discussed anyway." The motive, Knip suggested, was to protect the Chemical Weapons Convention; that is to say, that it was perceived to be better to have an incomplete convention rather than none at all, a view that seemed to imply that powerful signatories to the Convention had no intention of stalling the development of novichoks.

6   The likelihood that Skripal was a victim of Porton Down (whose history has included secret mass experiments on British citizens [Keys

2015]) or of British intelligence seems just as or even more probable than that he was attacked by Russia.

7   British government claims that applied or weaponized novichoks can only be military grade were also incorrect. Among relevant sources who attested to this was a leading British toxicologist, Alaistair Hay, at Leeds University, and a US scientist – Cornell University professor of organic chemistry, David Collum – who claimed that his graduate students could easily create novichoks in the university laboratory (Skwarkbox 2018). Had the novichoks truly been military-grade and of the much-vaunted potency claimed of them, it is more than curious that only three people were affected and that they all survived (although four months later there was an apparent casualty, Dawn Sturgess).

8   The behavior of the British government during the weeks immediately after the incident arguably demonstrated a lack of interest in and an incapacity/unwillingness to establish the truth. Examples include the "door handle" narrative in which the British government proposed that the poison had likely been applied to the front door handle to the Skripals' home, even though there was no guarantee that some third party might not have come into contact with the handle. Such a risky application would seem a curious decision for the deployment of a nerve agent into which millions of dollars of R&D had been invested and whose composition would then be exposed to the world and its future usefulness compromised. A BBC Panorama documentary in November 2018 (BBC 2018) indicated that the police still supported the door handle theory. Sources calculated that the poison had been applied/ sprayed around midday on Sunday March 4, while the Skripals were still at home, it was said, even though Sergei Skripal's office had a view directly on to the street and Skripal was reportedly acting in a nervous, anxious manner in the weeks leading up to the attempted assassination. In these circumstances, the likelihood that assassins could have approached the front door unopposed in order to conduct a delicate chemical weapons attack, under damp conditions thought by some (it is contested) to break down novichok, without being seen by the Skripals or by neighbors, was close to zero (Slane 2018). If the Skripals had actually been out at that time, they would have had to have returned, but there is no evidence for this. How would the assassins have been able to predict that both Julia and her father Sergei would touch the doorknob or, if they planned to attack only Sergei, how could they be sure that it be Sergei and not Julia who would touch the doorknob?

It did not become public knowledge until early 2019 that the very first responders were the chief nursing officer of the British Army, Alison McCourt, with experience in highly infectious disease (ebola), and her teenage daughter Abigail, who by an extraordinary coincidence were in the vicinity of the bench on which Sergei and Yulia had recently collapsed (Press Association 2019; RT 2019). The fact that none of the first responders (except possibly one – police detective sergeant Nick Baily, who was the third party injured and the first to recover), or helpers or other investigators were contaminated – even though some came into physical contact (CPR) with the victims and at least one of the victims may have vomited – and that all three of the initial victims recovered, raised alternative possibilities namely:

- That the poison was never A-234 in the first instance and that hospital and security services were lying or confused from the outset. For the first day they considered the opioid fentanyl a most likely cause, until according to some sources they were advised by the security services to consider a nerve agent as possibility. A-234 might have been inserted into samples following admission to hospital. Up to this time, neither first responders nor medical personnel appeared to use appropriate protective suits or to engage in the normal decontamination measures that accompany such use, such as a wash-down (Sushi 2018). Despite some press reports to the contrary no other members of the public were impacted at that time (although a number did seek medical reassurance that they had not been harmed). If novichok had broken down under damp conditions how was it that the OPCW were able to obtain traces of it that demonstrated high potency and purity?
- That the sample used against the Skripals contained some kind of "inhibitor" agent, perhaps NATO-produced BZ. Sources within OPCW's Swiss Spiez laboratory reportedly told Russian foreign secretary Sergey Lavrov that one of the samples sent to them to analyze – but possibly a control sample – contained BZ and A-234, a combination which might have delayed onset of the poison or simply incapacitated them for a period of time (Agence France Presse 2018). In another strange twist, the OPCW chairman publicly claimed that a relatively large quantity of the poison had been released – enough to wipe out a community – only to find himself contradicted by his own organization the following day.
- That the poison was from a deteriorating and therefore less potent sample from among those originally possessed by top Soviet scientist Leonid Rink (once in charge of Russia's novichok program) – as previously discussed – who is known to have sold several samples to Mafiosi figures of which one was used in 1995 to kill a prominent banker, Ivan Kivelidi and his chauffeur. Kivelidi

was the leader of the Russian Entrepreneurs' Round Table, an organization in conflict with a powerful group of directors of state-owned enterprises.

9 The cloistering of the Skripals from the press and from relatives, the refusal of a visa to a close relative (cousin) of Yulia Skripal's, the apparent lack of communication between Skripal and his mother, the refusal of the British government to provide ample and open information to the Russian government concerning the welfare of a Russian citizen (Yulia Skripal)(Janjevic 2018) and the alleged slapping of D- Notices on the British press to stop journalists reporting on at least certain aspects of the saga (especially details relating to Pablo Miller, Skripal's recruiter) are indicative of what may have been extreme embarrassment and duplicity at the most senior levels of the British state (Durden 2018a). In late May, a brief video interview with Yulia Skripal was publicly released. It appeared staged – possibly even coerced – filmed in an unknown location in which she talked about the pain of her experience, her wish to return to Russia eventually, and her decline of an offer of help from Russia (a statement that she theatrically signed on camera; Withers 2018). To the time of writing, Julia Skripal has not been seen or heard of in public since this interview, her father has not been seen or heard of in public at all and appears either not to have thought to contact his mother in Russia, is incapable of doing so, or has been counseled against or prevented from doing so. Nicholas Bailey, the policeman who was contaminated, has spoken of his experience on television.

10 Western media have constructed a narrative about Russian government predisposition to assassination, but on insufficient grounds. The killing by poison of former FSB spy Alexander Litvinenko in London in 2006 is often cited in this respect as though Russian government (even Putin) responsibility had been established beyond reasonable doubt. This is patently not the case. There was a public inquiry (not a court case as such) that blamed the Russian government, and even implicated Vladimir Putin (BBC 2016). The process and conclusions of this inquiry have attracted considerable criticism, and not only from Russia (Mercouris 2017). Russia was not involved in the inquiry and could not defend itself.

Litvinenko was one of 14 untimely deaths of Russian exiles in Britain that occurred over a period of ten years or so. Another was the death of Alexander Perepilichny in 2012. Media for years treated this death as a Kremlin murder (attributed to gelsemium, a poisonous herb). Anti-Putin financier Bill Browder (Heritage hedge fund) was among those who alleged that

Perepilichny could only have been murdered. Yet Surrey police did not find his death suspicious, putting it down to a heart attack suffered by an obese male after jogging. Two post-mortem examinations of the body failed to find a definite cause of death (Weiss 2018).

The answer to the question "who benefits," in such cases, arguably implicates the UK as much or more than Russia. High-profile exiles tend not to have good relations with the Russian government, sometimes on account of illegal activities they have conducted in Russia. It has been suggested that they are vulnerable to British pressure for them to denounce Russia and/or Putin and later, when their usefulness to the British has otherwise expired, may be eliminated in a manner that further supports the British anti-Russian campaign of vilification (Cunningham 2018b, c).

Further discourses about assassination in relation to Russia conveniently ignore a long history of assassination as a tool in the hands of Western intelligence agencies (MacAskill 2017). Prominent among them are assassinations committed by the British against the agents of former colonies, including Ireland, Kenya, Myanmar, Bahrain, and Yemen (identified by Curtis [2003]). In recent years it is western ally Israel that has carried out by far the largest number of assassinations – more than 800 (Bergman 2018). Hardly irrelevant is the staggering illegality and immorality of drone programs that routinely target victims (alleged "terrorists") for murder in numerous different "sovereign" countries on the basis only of "signature" data (i.e. no specific, individualized proof), attacks that regularly kill large numbers of innocent citizens (with the possibility that many more innocents have been killed by drone than actual "terrorists")(Zenco 2016).

7 Fake news and intelligence

Hacks and hackers

Alleged "hacking" of DNC/Clinton/Clinton Foundation/John Podesta emails by Russian spies

Special Counsel Robert Mueller issued indictments early 2018 against Russians and Russian institutions that he claimed were guilty of attempts to meddle with the US presidential election by means of bots and trolls (Special Counsel's Office 2018). He had not yet indicted the supposed perpetrators of the alleged hacking of DNC emails, even though the ICA and Steele dossiers indicated culpability of Russian intelligence. In all, he indicted 13 Russian nationals and three Russian companies on conspiracy charges. Some were also accused of identity theft. The charges specified a Russian propaganda effort to interfere with the 2016 campaign. The companies involved were the IRA, often described as a "Russian troll farm," and two companies that helped finance it. Russian nationals indicted included 12 of the agency's employees and its alleged financier, Yevgeny Prigozhin. These indictments were never likely to be tested in any court of law. In May 2017 Mueller's team appeared taken by surprise when Prigozhin showed himself ready to defend his companies (Brown 2018) and, when other attorneys began to demand discovery – which would have forced Mueller to reveal his (possibly shaky) evidence – things went quiet, and memory of the March indictments was shrouded in July by a set of new indictments focusing on the so-called hacking of the DNC emails. Many of Mueller's charges against members of the 2016 Trump campaign in some way implicated them in attempts to influence, access, or in some way benefit from the WikiLeaks publication of the emails, usually presumed to have been hacked by Russian intelligence. It is not obvious why, had there truly been collusion between the Trump campaign and Russia, Russia would not have provided the emails directly to the campaign but, arguably, the aim was to publicly embarrass the Democratic Party in a manner that would not implicate Trump.

The saga began well before the election, and resulted from the scandal of Clinton's use of a private server while she headed the State Department from 2009 to 2014 (Zurcher 2016). Clinton and her colleagues were condemned in July 2016 by FBI Director James Comey (Federal Bureau of Investigation 2018), following investigation, as "extremely careless in their handling of very sensitive, highly classified information." The "private server" scandal extended to the alleged deletion by Clinton of emails that were "personal," and the court-enforced publication of those that were State Department business. WikiLeaks published most of the latter following Freedom of Information (FoI) requests. Conflation of the "private server" scandal and the "DNC hack" scandal may account for missteps of those Trump campaign officials who hoped that further embarrassing revelations about Clinton would emerge in time to influence the election. The important takeaway point is that Clinton's opponents hoped that incriminating material would be unearthed amongst unpublished emails from her period as Secretary of State, or that related to the controversial Clinton Foundation, or that related to the conduct of the Democratic National Campaign from the start of the 2016 presidential election (Hicks 2016).

WikiLeaks published the leaked/hacked DNC emails in July 2016. Julian Assange denied that WikiLeaks received the emails from Russia. Here are the most important points to consider in assessing the significance of what occurred, or otherwise:

1   Scott Ritter (2016, 2017, 2018), quoting anonymous Dutch intelligence and press sources, reported that Dutch intelligence agents watched on their monitors as Russian hackers attacked a US State Department office with malware (APT29) in October 2014. The hackers were said to include both private citizens and intelligence agents. Dutch sources seemed certain that with the knowledge of Russian SVR intelligence, the DNC was hacked over 10 months using APT 29 from an office inside Moscow State University. Russian intelligence knew that the US knew (traces may have been left deliberately) and, from November 2014, concluded that the malware operation was no longer a deniable secret, so withdrew. The information they had collected was never "weaponized." The purpose may have been to demonstrate Russian capability and force US intelligence to take notice. The Dutch duly notified the FBI and NSA. A new APT29 team was discovered in mid-2015. Its targets included the DNC, but this had nothing to do with the hacking of DNC emails later published on WikiLeaks and was not linked to the Russian intelligence agency FSB as CrowdStrike claimed.

The FBI informed the DNC of the 2015 hack. The DNC took no action until April 2016, and, rather than allow the FBI to examine its servers or computers, hired a private cyber security research agency, CrowdStrike, to investigate. CrowdStrike's co-founder and CTO was Dmitri Alperovitch a nonresident senior fellow on the pro-NATO and anti-Russian think-tank, Atlantic Council. By this time the APT29 hackers were gone from DNC machines, and a new hacking entity appeared: APT28 or Fancy Bear. CrowdStrike monitored APT28, allowing it to access and exfiltrate documents that would later prove politically embarrassing. Then CrowdStrike and the DNC went public, attributing Fancy Bear to Russian military intelligence GRU. An outlier, independent journalist George Eliason, resident in the Donbass, has claimed that Fancy Bear was an anti-Russian operation answerable to Ukraine's Ministry of Information that sourced propaganda related to Ukrainian sites InformNapalm, Cyberhunta, and Myrotvorets (which Eliason charged with issuing international kill lists), and also a source, directly or indirectly, for Bellingcat.com and the Atlantic Council on a range of related anti-Russian issues concerning Ukraine, the downing of MH17 and Syria (Eliason 2018b).

Ritter argued that CrowdStrike had no hard evidence of Russian involvement when briefing the press in June 2016. While claims of Russian origination were supported by the ICA in 2017 and other establishment sources, actual public evidence has been thin, hedged in "likely" and "consistent with" vocabulary. An IP address in the malware previously cited as evidence of Russian involvement was a false trail. By the time of CrowdStrike's investigation any hacker could have accessed the APT28 toolset (since it had "gone wild"). Were "tracks" deliberately inserted into evidence to make it look as though Russia was culpable even though the perpetrator was actually somebody else (most likely US intelligence)? In the wake of the Snowden 2013 revelations of NSA surveillance techniques, US intelligence clearly possessed capability to plant tracks (Macaskill and Dance 2013), a capability perhaps refined by 2016. NSA terminated its policy under section 702 of the Foreign Intelligence Surveillance Act (FISA) that had allowed it to search all Internet data passing through its computers for certain search terms and to collect that data if any part of the communication passed outside of the US, even if one or both parties to the conversation were Americans (Kiriakou 2018). NSA continued to collect communications coming from or going to a foreign national. Warrantless Internet surveillance continues as surely do many of the other abuses identified by Snowden.

Then "Guccifer 2.0" emerged. The original Guccifer, a Romanian hacker claiming to have penetrated the private emails of Hillary Clinton was subsequently imprisoned in the USA. Guccifer 2.0 dismissed charges of Russian attribution, asserting that he alone was responsible for the DNC server hack. As "proof," he published documents sourced, apparently, to the DNC server. Some of these were copied using a template embedding a Cyrillic text into the published documents' metadata, including the name of the KGB's founder, Felix Dzerzhinsky. The ICA report of January 2017 concluded that Guccifer 2.0 was a Russian agent. US intelligence subsequently claimed that Guccifer 2.0 neglected to switch on VPN cover on one occasion, exposing his real location as Moscow, not Romania (Price and Sheth 2018), a very unprofessional mistake, if so. Later analysis by the widely respected *Forensicator* concluded that Guccifer 2:0's consistent intent was to plant clues which connected it to Russia (Durden 2018e), indicating that Guccifer 2:0 might have been a western intelligence operation.

As in many Western allegations of malfeasance against Russia, Russia is presented as having a *penchant* for implausibly incriminating tracks. Guccifer 2:0 resurfaced in Mueller's indictments of July 2018, asserting that: Guccifer 2:0 was run by the GRU, NSA had been alerted by British intelligence to Guccifer's running of DNC materials, Julian Assange had requested that Guccifer 2:0 send DNC materials to WikiLeaks, and Guccifer 2:0 had established contacts with Americans who may not have known it was connected to Russia or Russian intelligence. These Americans reportedly included an employee working for Brietbart News under Steve Bannon, and Roger Stone, an informal advisor to Donald Trump who later declared that he considered the DNC materials were leaked not hacked. The DNC supposedly became aware of the alleged hack on April 19, 2016, but the worst of it may have occurred in the subsequent three days. The first stolen documents were made public by Guccifer 2:0 on June 15. Some of the materials were re-published on American websites (Sanger et al 2018).

2   Metadata released by Guccifer 2:0 indicated transfer speeds consistent with an internal source at DNC copying the files (see following text), rather than external exfiltration (Lawrence 2017; Various 2017). While US intelligence (ODNI 2017) claimed that methods and IP addresses were "consistent with" Russian state hackers, Ritter (2017) skeptically argued that they were also "consistent with" almost every other hacker. Several sources (notably Craig Murray, VIPS, and Kim DotCmm) debunk the hacking theories, finding instead that there were no hackings, only insider leaks. WikiLeaks denied that its material came from Russia (McCarthy 2017). Although Assange may have been hostile to Clinton (Mackey 2017), WikiLeaks had a good reputation for protecting sources. The notion that Assange impugned its track record was nurtured incorrectly by a CNN story that Donald Trump and his son Donald Trump Jnr had received a web address and decryption key allowing them to access hacked documents from WikiLeaks before these were publicly available (Darcy 2017), and to earlier stories of correspondence between Assange and Trump Jnr, in which

WikiLeaks's questions to Trump appeared pro-Trump and anti-Clinton (Tracy 2017b).

So, was it a hack? The Mueller indictments of July 2018 asserted that it was. At least five sources say it wasn't, of which at least the first three are significant:

Craig Murray, former British ambassador and friend of Julian Assange. Murray said he retrieved the package from a source during a clandestine meeting in a wooded area near American University, in northwest D.C. He said the individual he met with was not the original person who obtained the information, but an intermediary (Shaw 2016; Murray 2017).

Members of Veteran Intelligence Professionals for Sanity (VIPS). They believed they had demonstrated that the speed of downloads could only have been achieved by means of a direct memory stick. The chief VIPS researchers active on the DNC case were four: William Binney, formerly NSA's technical director for world geopolitical and military analysis and designer of many agency programs now in use; Kirk Wiebe, formerly a senior analyst at NSA's SIGINT Automation Research Center; Edward Loomis, formerly technical director in NSA's Office of Signal Processing; and Ray McGovern, an intelligence analyst for nearly three decades and formerly chief of the CIA's Soviet Foreign Policy Branch. The four argued that NSA's known programs were fully capable of capturing all electronic transfers of data and of determining whether or not hacking has occurred. VIPS data undermined the credibility of Guccifer 2:0 and assigned him to irrelevancy. VIPS research also showed that whoever entered the DNC system did so from the Eastern USA, and that the alleged "Russian" traces, were actually inserted after posting.

At least two members of the VIPS team believed that the "Russian did it" meme was a deliberate diversion instigated by the DNC, possibly with the aid of the CIA and its "Marble" toolkit, to avert public attention from the evidence of favoritism shown by the DNC during the primaries, and Clinton's buddy relationships to Wall Street that would be disclosed in the DNC emails once these were published by WikiLeaks. Assange gave notice on June 12, 2016 that he was about to do so (they were published by WikiLeaks on July 22). The DNC had sufficient time to concoct a defense in the form of CrowdStrike's claim on June 14 to have found Russian malware, and Guccifer 2:0's claim on June 15 to have been responsible for the "hack."

The VIPS analysis derived from data provided by a source *Forensicator* said to be connected to an analyst writing under the pseudonym Adam Carter. *Forensicator* later showed that the document uploaded by Guccifer 2:0 on June 15 came not from Russia but from the USA (McGovern 2018a).

Disagreement with VIPS claims came from within VIPS itself (Lawrence 2017; Various 2017). Dissenters argued not that exfiltration of the kind described was impossible but that other explanations were also plausible. Dissenters testified that data-transfer speeds across networks and the Internet could easily achieve rates that greatly exceeded the cited reference in the VIPS report, depending on the capacity of the network and the method of access to it. Further, the data transfer could have happened on a server separate from the DNC or elsewhere, with data previously copied, transferred, or even exfiltrated from the DNC.

In response, authors of the original VIPS memo argued that the DNC server had to have been accessed at some point, that the dissenters overlooked the difference between available speeds in early July 2016 and those available in summer 2018, and that the dissenters' argument failed to take into account degradation of speed with distance, or the problem of transoceanic connections. Further, dissenters had ignored the fact that on July 5, the data was transferred at a speed not obtainable from East Coast ISPs, while being entirely consistent with a USB port connected to a portable device such as a thumb drive.

The Nation's independent analyst Nicholas Freitas deemed that while the work of *Forensicator* had been "detailed and accurate" there were many ways in which the high speed of data transfer could have been achieved and that the theory of the fabrication of Russian fingerprints could not be confirmed with certainty. However, many sources in support of the "hacking" theory depend on their presumption that the hack was conducted by Guccifer 2:0 on behalf of Russian intelligence. *Forensicator*'s evidence suggests that most of Guccifer 2:0's modifications to metadata were deliberate: the process which Guccifer 2:0 used to plant Russian error messages was complex and deliberate – across 36 documents published in several batches, each batch with a metadata change. A metadata change only "sticks" if a document is modified and then saved; Guccifer's document modifications were minimal, unnecessary, and trivial.

John Solomon, an investigative journalist writing for The Hill, reported in June 2018 that following extensive investigation there was evidence of a draft deal in early 2017 between Julian Assange and the Justice Department, also involving the participation of James Comey, then director of the FBI, and the Vice-Chair of the Senate Select Committee on Intelligence, Senator Mark Warner (a principal player in Russia-Gate fear-mongering). The deal would have given Assange "limited immunity" allowing him to leave the Ecuadorian embassy in London in exchange for Assange's undertaking to provide a measure of protection to the CIA in any further WikiLeaks releases of CIA-related classified documents. Assange also offered "to discuss technical evidence ruling out certain parties in the controversial leak of Democratic Party emails to WikiLeaks during the 2016 election," which Solomon and others clearly believe would have confirmed Assange's previous insistence that Russia was not party to the leak (not hack). Very soon thereafter negotiators were informed of Comey's direction that they "stand down," and the deal collapsed, soon to be followed by Assange's release of the "Vault 7" files. These included information as to the CIA's *Marble Framework* tool, enabling the agency to "hack into computers, disguise who hacked in, and falsely attribute the hack to someone else by leaving so-called tell-tale signs – like Cyrillic, for example". The CIA documents also showed that the *Marble* tool had been employed in 2016 (McGovern 2018a, d).

Kim Dotcom, a German-Finnish Internet entrepreneur who lives in New Zealand, was a teen hacker offering an encrypted services site known as megaupload.com (now closed). He claimed he could get Clinton's deleted emails. Dotcom also claimed that Seth Rich provided the material to WikiLeaks, but this claim has been roundly contested by many sources including investigators into Rich's murder, his parents, and the proponents of the hacking theory including Special Counsel Robert Mueller. Dotcom made several related comments and tweets hinting at upcoming email releases prior to the WikiLeaks dumps (Syrmopoulos 2018).

John Mark Dougan, a former West Palm Beach County cop, who also ran several dissident and whistleblower websites, has claimed he was contacted by Seth Rich in February of 2016, that he received a thumb drive containing the DNC emails from Rich and delivered these indirectly to Assange (Goodman 2018). But the same strong doubts apply as for Kim Dotcom.

These considerations notwithstanding, in July 2018 and as part of special counsel Robert Mueller's investigation into Russian interference and links between the Trump campaign and Moscow, a federal grand jury charged 12 Russian intelligence officers with hacking Democratic computer networks in 2016. Hackers working for GRU, the indictments claimed, had used false online personas, "spearphishing" and keystroke loggers to access and monitor activity on 33 DNC computers in 2016. They also laundered money, targeted a State election board, and stole private voter information on about 500,000 voters. They released stolen documents to DCLeaks, and Guccifer 2.0 and ultimately to WikiLeaks. The narrative of these indictments contained no actual evidence (this may change if and when the Mueller report is published in 2019). Hornberger (2018b) noted skeptically that "a prosecutor can say whatever he wants in an indictment. It's not sworn to. Neither the prosecutor nor the grand jury can be prosecuted for perjury or false allegations in an indictment." Despite this, western mainstream media almost universally leaped on the indictments as though they were proof of something:

> An indictment is not evidence; it is simply the formal notice to the defendants of the charges against each of them. The mere fact of an indictment raises no suspicion of guilt. The government has the burden to prove the charges against the defendants beyond a reasonable doubt, and that burden stays with the government from start to finish. The defendants have no burden or obligation to prove anything at all. They are presumed innocent. The defendants started this trial with a clean slate, with no evidence at all against them, and the law presumes that they are each innocent. This presumption of innocence stays with each defendant unless and until the government presents evidence here in court that overcomes the presumption, and convinces you beyond a reasonable doubt that the defendants are guilty.
>
> (Hornberger 2018b)

A significant problem in the event that these charges would be addressed in open court with an alert defense team was that the FBI had allowed a private third party company, Crowdstrike, to conduct its own investigation. The FBI itself had investigated nothing.

> If this dubious information, sourced from an unaccountable third party never placed under oath with numerous reasons to lie or at least mislead, was used as evidential basis for any indictment, that indictment cannot stand up in court. . . . CrowdStrike delivers geopolitically-actionable conclusions swaddled in just enough technical jargon to dissuade observers from looking too closely.
>
> (Buyniski 2018)

Scott Ritter was skeptical about the leap of logic required to get from the inner workings of the servers of the Democratic Party to the offices of Russian intelligence officers in Moscow – a link that Ritter judged was not backed up by anything that demonstrated how these connections were made. Nor did he think the government would ever be able to demonstrate them in a court of law because it would have to produce the specific evidence link- ing the hacks to the named Russians, and provide details on how this evi- dence was collected, and by whom. But this would reveal some of the most sensitive sources and methods of intelligence collection by the US intelli- gence community. Additionally, the indictments suggested greater certainty than the facts actually allowed. Citing an NSA document of alleged Russian penetration of state and county election offices, Ritter noted that the NSA was far more circumspect than the special counsel's team. The indictment had taken detailed data and "shoehorned it into the organizational chart of a military intelligence unit assessed – but not known – to have overseen the operations described" (Ritter 2018a, c).

3   Perhaps more significant than any of this, from the perspective of a concern for the integrity of the US electoral system, is what was in the emails namely, evidence (some Sanders' supporters might argue) that the DNC "rigged" the primaries to favor Clinton over Bernie Sanders and that Clinton received large sums from Wall Street audiences for speeches whose texts were not publicly available and that were at vari- ance with her campaign promises (Berman 2016; Klein 2017).

4   Much of the substance of alleged collusion between Trump Campaign advisers and Russians had to do with efforts to get access to the materi- als that WikiLeaks eventually published before they were published. This very much is the case with respect to George Papadopoulos (a jun- ior foreign policy advisor to the Trump campaign) and Maltese Profes- sor Joseph Mifsud who told Papadopoulos that he could get him access to hacked emails from Russia. Mifsud, who ran a school for diplomacy in London, now closed, was originally assumed to have been a Russian spy but may have been as closely related to western as to Russian intel- ligence (Vos 2018a; Vos 2018b).

Several people seem to have been aware of the upcoming WikiLeaks dump before it happened. Since WikiLeaks gave two weeks' notice of intent, prior knowledge of a release was hardly a surprise, although prior knowledge of the content of the emails to be released would have been. Those with *apparent* prior knowledge either of hacked/leaked materials themselves or of an intended WikiLeaks release included the CEO of Cam- bridge Analytica (who asked WikiLeaks if Analytica could help sort out the emails); Joseph Mifsud (possible Russian or US intelligence) and his dis- closure to George Papadopoulos; Roger Stone (Trump friend and advisor); and Roger Smith (Trump friend and advisor). Whatever the involvement of Russian intelligence (and there may have been no such involvement) certain figures within or close to the Trump campaign were salivating at the thought of acquiring or determining the subject matter and release dates of hacked/leaked emails.

Mueller-related prosecutors have alleged that a man – now known to be Mifsud – told Papadopoulos in late April 2016 – about two months before leaked emails began appearing online – that the Kremlin had "dirt" on Hillary Clinton, Trump's rival, and was secretly sitting on "thousands of emails" covertly hacked from the Democratic Party. Papdaopoulos passed this information on to the Australian ambassador Alexander Downer.

> Downer is closely tied with The Clinton Foundation via his role in securing $25 million in aid from his country to help the Clinton Foundation fight AIDS. He is also a member of the advisory board of London-based Hakluyt & Co, an opposition research and intelligence firm set up in 1995 by three former UK intelligence officials and described as 'a retirement home for ex-MI6 [British foreign intelligence] officers', but it now also recruits from the worlds of management consultancy and banking.
>
> (Vos 2018b)

Downer informed Australian intelligence of his conversation with Papadopoulos and Australian Intelligence in turn, after two months' delay, informed the FBI. This started an FBI investigation in July 2016. (The FBI met with Steele in October – Steele had shared some of his findings with an FBI agent three months earlier, which would have been in July). Mifsud appeared to have high level Russian connections, particularly to Ivan Timofeev, program director of the academic Valdai Discussion Club. Mifsud has even been called an agent for SVR. But Mifsud's alleged links to Russian intelligence are put into some doubt by his close working relationship with Claire Smith, a major figure in the upper echelons of British intelligence (according to an investigative report by Elizabeth Vos 2018b). WikiLeaks Editor-in-Chief Julian Assange likewise noted the connection between Mifsud and Smith in a Twitter thread (additionally pointing out his connections with Saudi intelligence):

> [Mifsud] and Claire Smith of the UK Joint Intelligence Committee and eight-year member of the UK Security Vetting panel both trained Italian security services at the Link University in Rome and appear to both be present in this [photo].
>
> (Vos 2018b)

Vos reported that Claire Smith was training military and law enforcement officials alongside Mifsud in 2012 during her tenure as a member of the UK

Cabinet Office Security Vetting Appeals Panel, which oversees the vetting process for UK intelligence placement. This indicates that Mifsud may have been incorrectly characterized as a Russian intelligence asset, since it is unlikely that Claire Smith's role in vetting UK intelligence personnel would lead to her accidentally working with a Russian agent. Mifsud's working relationship with Claire Smith suggested a direct connection to UK intelligence, given Smith's membership of the UK's Joint Intelligence Committee (JIC), a supervisory body overseeing all UK intelligence agencies. The JIC is part of the Cabinet Office and reports directly to the Prime Minister. The Committee also sets the collection and analysis priorities for all of the agencies it supervises. Claire Smith also served as a member of the UK's Cabinet Office (Vos 2018b).

5   Just as charges of Russian "election meddling" pale into insignificance when compared to the infinitely broader history of US meddling in the elections of other nations, so charges of Russian "hacking" pale into insignificance when considered against the global reach and sophistication of NSA surveillance as demonstrated in the Edward Snowden leaks from 2013 onwards. Among these revelations, as an article in *Intercept* has explained, is that the NSA can infect computers with "implants" that allow the NSA to siphon out data from foreign Internet and phone networks. In some cases, the NSA has masqueraded as a fake Facebook server using the social media site as a launching pad to infect a target's computer and exfiltrate files from a hard drive (Gallagher and Greenwald 2014; Couts 2014). An automated system – Turbine (operational since 2010) – is designed to allow the implant networks to scale to large size. One implant plug-in codenamed UNITDRAKE enables the NSA to gain total control of an infected computer. Other implants can record conversations, snap photos, record browsing histories, collect log-in details and passwords, and log key-strokes. They have the power to modify content of data packets that are passing between computers (ibid). Hannan notes that the "NSA's ability to follow hacking to its exact source is a matter of public record. Yet there is still no opposition to hysteria about 'Russian' hacking. But Russiagate is useful because it normalizes far-reaching censorship" (Hannan 2018). The list of the CIA's cyber-tools that WikiLeaks began to release in March 2017 labeled Vault 7 included *Marble* that is capable of obfuscating the origin of documents in false-flag operations and leaving markings that point to whatever the CIA wants to point to. (The tool can also "de-obfuscate" what it has obfuscated; Lawrence 2017). It is not known whether this tool was deployed in the Guccifer 2:0 case, but it exists for such a use (Goldman 2018).

8 RussiaGate and the Russian "threat"

EurAsia, key to global dominance

Here I shall relate RussiaGate discourse to the perceived or manufactured Russian "threat." Understanding of RussiaGate requires appeal to a longer history of relations between the USA and Russia and of Russia with other competing imperial powers. Behind perceptions of Russia lie western concerns about China.

Western hostility to Russia has nearly always been refracted in Russian eyes, not in a matching intensity of hostility, but in a curious hybrid of hurt outrage and continuing admiration for what educated Russians perhaps regrettably regard as a civilization that is more advanced than theirs. The western threat to Russia was evident in western interventions against Russia by the French emperor Napoleon Bonaparte, western invasions, or covert actions against the Soviet Union in support of "White Russians" during and for some time following World War I, and Hitler's invasion of Russia during World War II in 1941. Later stages of this history include:

> Anti-Soviet maneuverings by the Intelligence communities after World War 2, including US election meddling against sympathetic Communist parties in France, Greece, Italy, in particular, and maneuvers against Socialist parties in Britain and Australia, among others (Blum 2004).

> The hysterically anti-Soviet and anti-Communist McCarthy era in the USA 1950–54.

> Anti-Soviet maneuverings, persisting with varying levels of intensity, throughout the (first) Cold War, 1947–91.

> Direct confrontations as over Cuba, which precipitated the Cuban "missile crisis," nearly erupting in nuclear war in 1962; and less direct but

equally or even more devastating confrontations as in Angola during the civil war from 1975, Vietnam 1955–75, and Afghanistan 1979–1989;

The opposition of neo-conservatives (such as Leo Strauss, Bill Kristol, Donald Rumsfeld, Dick Cheney, Paul Wolfowitz) from the Reagan years onwards to policies of détente, and their establishment of parallel intelligence structures that could more easily be politicized than the CIA or NSA to supply pretexts for war (Heilbrunn 2008).

Western facilitation of the disintegration of the Soviet Union and support for the first President of the Russian Federation, Boris Yeltsin (1991–1998) (McFaul 2005).

The West's role in the disintegration of the Socialist Federal Republic of Yugoslavia (1989–2008) (Herman and Peterson 2007).

In his book *In the Shadows of the American Century*, Alfred McCoy reminded readers that for over 100 years EurAsia has been identified by geopolitical strategists as the key to global dominance for would-be imperial powers (McCoy 2017). Such is the case of the works of Halford Mackinder (1904), Elihu Root (1900 to 1916/2019), George Kennan (founder of containment theory, 1940s) and Zbigniew Brezenzinski (1990s). A significant feature of the US style of imperialism that McCoy identified in his analysis of US policing of the Philippines during the first half of the 20th century is its heavy reliance on the co-option and nurture of local power (including measures of regime-change when necessary), penetration and manipulation of (especially) opposition movements, and the spread of military bases and covert operations in addition to military force (McCoy 2009). The limits of this approach are tested by nuclear weapons, as became evident in the case of the Soviet Union after World War 2, the Cuban missile crisis of 1962, and China from 1964. The proliferation of nuclear weapons has been tolerated by the USA when this has occurred among its allies (including the UK, France and Israel, extending more recently to India and Pakistan), but detested when it has involved opponents (most notably, North Korea) and exploited as leverage for regime change in the case of opponent states that could be charged with possessing nuclear weapon "programs" even on the flimsiest evidence (see the cases of Iraq 2003 and Libya 2011 as discussed in Boyd-Barrett 2015) or where there is actually no evidence at all (see the case of Iran as discussed in Boyd-Barrett 2015).

From the point of view of consolidating world hegemony, globalization and the discipline of the World Trade Organization was a huge strategic blunder of US neo-liberalism, welcome as it may have been from other points of view, facilitating as it did the rapid ascent of China as a Communist-driven system of industrial capitalism that has sorely strained the prospects of US global economic hegemony. In turn it has fostered a US neo-conservative retreat to nationalistic, militaristic solutions for the preservation of US hegemony. While the longer-term likelihood of success is dubious at best, this is advantageous to neo-conservatism in the short term, because it props up the incubus of the military-industrial-intelligence apparatus. This requires an economy of permanent war for its survival. It does not matter that its wars are won or lost – indeed, a strategic state of military "loss" is actually beneficial for such an economy, so long as it does not undermine image and morale. It further justifies policies of domestic repression and militarism that serve to ensure the continued flow of tax-payer dollars to the incubus. It facilitates policies of internal exploitation (including intensification of anti-immigrant and racist policies, deregulation of environment protections, deregulation of banking and finance, wage suppression and theft, voter suppression, elimination of social benefits, market concentration, undermining or cooption of trades unions, removal of workplace protections, supremely expensive yet mediocre healthcare, privatization of prisons, murderous use of police force, and debtor prisons) which serve to siphon the wealth of the masses to the elites and to keep them under the heel of monopoly capitalism.

While still dwarfed by US military and economic power China had emerged as a far greater objective, long-term threat to US interests in the 2000s than Russia in competition for EurAsia and the world. This was due, not least, to the amazingly rapid development of China's One Belt One Road policy, to say nothing of its long, slow encroachment of diplomatic and trading influence throughout Africa, Latin America, and the Middle East. This development occurred with the active or passive consent of Russia. The post–Cold War Sino-Russian axis was seeded when Chinese President Jiang Zemin conferred with Boris Yeltsin in Moscow, 1997, resulting in the "Joint Declaration on a Multipolar World and the Establishment of a New International Order," signed some 18 months before Putin became President of Russia (Klare 2018).

Chinese power is potentially clipped by greater western control over Moscow. But when the west pushes hard against Russia, Russia inclines towards China and this reduces the long-term likelihood that western (US) hegemony can survive. Yet neoconservative policy has erred in this direction since the fall of Yeltsin, perhaps inspired by its over-optimistic belief in regime-change/color revolution strategies that have served western interests so often in the past. Arguably this approach invests excessive confidence in the influence of the Moscow intelligentsia and those oligarchs who do not submit to the Kremlin's requirement that they support its political machine of managed democracy. There may be an encrusted bias in the US intelligence community that favors skepticism as to the possibility of a Sino-Russian alliance. Writing for the *Financial Times*, Jamil Anderlini (2018) warned that "the West ignores the alliance forming between Moscow and Beijing at its peril." Cooperation between the two countries included Russian supply of crude oil to China (China's biggest supplier in 2017); Chinese loans of tens of billions of dollars to Moscow to secure future oil and gas supplies, and the two countries' close military relationship.

Perhaps unwittingly, the rise of Trump and his (initially) pro-Russian sentiments (regardless of their cause) constituted a threat to this (failing) strategy and, left to his own devices, Trump might have inserted a wedge between Moscow and Beijing that in turn could have weakened both powers relative to the USA. Indeed it was reported in July 2018 that Nixon's former national security adviser Henry Kissinger had held several private meetings with Trump during the presidential transition, in which

> the foreign-policy veteran suggested that Trump pursue his anti-China agenda by improving the U.S.'s overall strategic position through a series of diplomatic overtures that would see Washington build closer relations to Russia – as well as India, Japan, the Philippines, and Middle Eastern nations, among others – in order to counter the perceived threat China poses to U.S. imperialist hegemony.
>
> (Gabriel 2018)

Under the administrations of both Obama and Trump the USA has exercised a concerted drive to link the Indian and Pacific Oceans and so encircle China with pro-American, anti-Chinese alliance systems, an area covering about 50% of the Earth's surface and incorporating more than half of the global population (Klare 2018), a measure which China will resist in whatever way it can. Beyond Kissinger, however, Trump may even have committed his administration (without the support of America's foreign policy establishment) to the concept of a tri-polar order, described by Klare (2018) as a model in which Russia, China, and the USA would each assume responsibility for maintaining stability within their own respective spheres of influence while cooperating to resolve disputes wherever those spheres overlap.

Both Democrats and Republicans, since the fall of the Soviet Union (which the USA helped orchestrate and whose transition to capitalism – catastrophic in many ways for most Russians – was guided in significant measure by western financiers, advisers, and ideologues), have consistently pushed for greater influence over Moscow by means of gradual regime change operations in the countries of the Former Soviet Union, with a likely view to the ultimate collapse of the Putin regime and the opening up of Russian wealth to unfettered western capitalist development. Trump's approach, by contrast, might be seen either as (1) a selfish bid to buddy up with Putin and the oligarchs, take as much as he can for himself and "screw the rest"; or, as Klare (2018a, b) has suggested (2), a more principled awareness of the advantages to the USA of a tri-polar world in which Russia and China are seen as competitors to the USA but not as existential enemies, liberating the USA of its inherited, expensive and increasingly dangerous neoliberal mission to lead the planet and intervene wherever its leadership is contested.

At a less elevated but significant level of consideration in the battle for Central Asian wealth is the role of Russia as a significant global supplier of fossil fuel energy. Ahmed (2018) quoted US Army's Command and General Staff College Press of the Combined Arms Center at Fort Leavenworth, prepared by US Army's Culture, Regional Expertise, and Language Management Office. The document makes it clear that the basic US goal is to dominate Central Asian oil and gas resources and acknowledges that the "driving force is Russian militarism." While Russia has significant leverage in this domain (often encouraging western energy companies to seek partnership with Russian) Russia also has significant vulnerabilities. For example, the Baku-Tbilisi-Ceyhan (BTC) pipeline was the first major pipeline from the Caspian to bypass Russian territory; another is the Trans-Afghan online project (TAPI) being built after more than 20 years of meddling. The west has established its interests in Turkmenistan, Kazakhstan, Uzbekistan, and Tajikstan, which together have fabulous oil, natural gas, uranium, gold, hydroelectricity – these are all being absorbed into the US-dominated market economy.

Despite enormous pushback from the USA and some of its European allies, Russia has continued to make progress along with German and four other European partners with Nord Stream 2, and to reduce its dependence on Ukraine as a country of passage for its oil and gas pipelines. The EU had more success in meddling with Russia's South Stream project through the farce of the Third Energy Package's seemingly anti-monopoly measure whose real purpose was to force Russia to remove Gazprom's control over its own pipeline. Although South Stream was abandoned in 2014 (Russia canceled it rather than agree to EU's condition with respect to Gazprom), it was well on the way to resurrection in 2018 in the wake of improved relations between Russia and Turkey and the prospect of a return to the participation of Bulgaria.

In addition to becoming a major energy supplier to China, the core of Russia's coexistence strategy with China's One Belt One Road is its leadership role alongside China in building alternative coalitions to the US-dominated political and economic system, principally the Shanghai Cooperation Organization

(SCO), BRICS, and the Eurasian Customs Union (ECU) (ibid). Ahmed identified an important link between Russian energy wealth and its weapons. He argued that the Kremlin is

> using its nuke arsenal as a strategic reserve to protect its smaller conventional force while relying on unconventional and asymmetric methods to secure national interests. Without physical buffers Western expansion towards Moscow eliminates Moscow's ability to "trade space for time."
>
> (Ahmed 2018a)

Is Russia a threat to the west?

Hardly. In terms of its economy, population, and military expenditure, Russia is clearly not a threat. Russia's military expenditure actually declined by 20% in 2017 to $61 billion and was forecast to fall further (Kottasová 2018). US expenditure of $610 billion (set to rise by another $100 billion in 2018), accounted for 35% of global military expenditure ($1.7 trillion; Cebul 2018). Russia was fourth largest spender, after Saudi Arabia. Russia aimed to restrict overall military expenditure to less than 3% of national GDP, less than the USA's 2016 rate of 3.3% and a lot less than Saudi Arabia's 10% (Brennan 2018).

Russia's population of 160 million is barely half of the USA's 300 million and a humble fraction of China's 1.4 billion. Most of Russia is uninhabited: 22 people per sq. mile. Its economy is insufficiently diversified. It depended on oil and gas for 8–14% of GDP in the period 2000–2016. This industry is in turn heavily dependent on complex networks of pipelines that require enormous investment and difficult political negotiations with multiple countries (whose attitudes towards Russia are volatile) in order to distribute its products safely to key customers throughout Europe and Asia (Global Economy 2018). Yeltsin's immense theft on behalf of cronies and in response to western financial interests in the 1990s destroyed the great gains of the USSR and plunged most of the country's people into deep poverty from which they began to recover under Putin (Tennison 2018).

The Soviet Union's 1979 invasion of Afghanistan (in response to a request for help from the Kabul government at the time) notwithstanding, its successor state – the Russian Federation – has not demonstrated strong aggression internationally, other than an invasion of Georgia in 2008 to protect its alliance with the breakaway regions of South Ossetia and Abkhazia whose autonomy came under military threat from Georgia. Russia's interventions in Ukraine (2014) and Syria (2015) were acts of defense (to protect warm-water ports of Sevastopol, and Tortus). The USA, by contrast, has 40 warm water bases on its own territory and 31 naval bases across the world (McCoy 2018).

In Ukraine, the transfer of Crimea to Russia occurred only after referenda approved the secession of Crimea from Ukraine, and after the request that Russia re-absorb Crimea. Crimea has a majority Russian-speaking and Russophile population, many of its principal cities are heavily populated by Russian military personnel and their families, and many independent surveys continue to show that the secession from Ukraine is still approved by the majority of people in Crimea. In the Donbass of Eastern Ukraine, Russia remained detached in the sense that it did not respond to requests that it absorb the Donbass, knowing that in the Donbass there was much less interest in joining Russia than had been the case in Crimea. There have been strong demands in the Donbass for greater autonomy within the political structure of Ukraine, a form of de-centralization called for by the international Minsk agreements to which Russia is a signatory, and yet are still resolutely opposed by Kiev under pressure from its "radical nationalists" (fascists). One source of opposition to Russia in Crimea – the Muslim Tatars – is not particularly happy with either Russia or Ukraine (see Boyd-Barrett 2017 for an extensive discussion of the Ukraine crisis).

In Syria Russia has played an immensely positive role. A South Front assessment notes that one of the key reasons behind the Russian operation in Syria was concern over security threats from terrorist groups near Russia's southern borders and the possibility that some powers could exploit terrorist groups in the larger, ongoing geopolitical standoff (SouthFront 2018). Until Russia's intervention, the USA appeared not to be effectively engaged against the forces of ISIS. The USA bears significant culpability for the rapid emergence of ISIS from 2004, dating back at least to the decision of the George W. Bush administration and its occupying force to dissolve the Baa'thist administration and Iraqi army in 2003 (Thompson 2015). This came atop of a much longer and more complex history of US-UK-French exploitation of fundamentalist Islamic, Muslim Brotherhood, and Saudi government-supported and financed Wahhabi movements (Benjamin 2016) to combat nationalist, communist, and socialist opposition to imperial interest (Curtis 2018, Davidson 2016; see also Bennis 2015, Cockburn 2015). US combat against ISIS in Syria was desultory in contrast to its energy in Iraq. The USA had installed the puppet government of Iraq following its invasion and occupation from 2003. But in Syria the larger goal, that dates back long before the supposed outbreak of civil war in 2011, was regime change to topple the Baa'thist (socialist and secular) regime of Bashar Al-Assad (Gowans 2017). This goal has been pursued through many proxy forces from Europe, Turkey, Saudi Arabia, the UAE, Qatar, and supposedly "moderate" anti-Assad (i.e. anti-socialist and anti-secular)

Jihadists, relatively few of them native to Syria, and many affiliated directly or indirectly with Al Qaeda or Al-Qaeda offspring such as Al Nusra. Further impediments to a determined US push against ISIS in Syria were economic and political alliances and covert dealings between ISIS and corporate interest from a number of countries. These were illustrated by the investigations of Franco-Swiss cement and construction firm Lafarge on charges of "financing terrorism" over its ties to ISIS. Dubois (2018) charged that

> French government and business circles financed and defended ISIS in a war for regime change targeting Syrian President Bashar al-Assad, while denouncing it as terrorist to the population. . . . Lafarge had made financial deals with terrorist groups including ISIS and the Al Qaeda-linked Al Nusra Front in 2012–2014, handing $15 million to ISIS in "donations," "taxes" and "commissions." Lafarge also brought petrochemicals from ISIS and raw materials for cement from ISIS-held mines. . . . Lafarge was constantly in touch with French intelligence officials in Syria and worked with them so closely that it seems impossible to delineate their cement-making from their intelligence activities.
>
> (Dubois 2018)

Serious roll-back of ISIS began only with the arrival of Russia. In addition, Russian diplomacy helped combat and defuse US and West European efforts to exploit (false) allegations that Assad had deployed chemical weapons against Jihadists in East Ghouta in 2013 as a pretext for direct western invasion (Boyd-Barrett 2015). Russia has continued to play an immensely valuable role in the stabilization of Syria, the maintenance in power of Assad (who continued to win legitimate, competitive presidential elections throughout the civil war), and the return of very large populations of Syrians to their homes following the defeat of ISIS forces in cities such as Aleppo.

Russia's answer to NATO – the Collective Security Treaty Organization – has not gained traction. Yet NATO – principally representing the interests of the USA, which provides most of its funds, and the European Union – has shown considerable aggressive intent against Russia by absorbing countries of the former Soviet Union and of the former Soviet bloc in Eastern Europe into NATO and/or the European Union. Eastwards NATO pressure arrived at the borders of the Russian federation with the US-supported coup d'etat against an elected regime in Ukraine in 2013. The eastwards march of the EU/NATO violates the western assurances given the last Soviet president, Mikhail Gorbachev, as testified by numerous documents compiled by the National Security Archive (2017).

One should further recall that the configuration of the Soviet Union and its sphere of influence in Communist Eastern Europe was conceded by US

President Roosevelt and UK Prime Minister Winston Churchill at the Yalta Agreements of 1944 (Latin Library nd).

Russia's relationship with China has deepened, but China's "Belt and Road Initiative" (BRI) runs through Russia's historical area of influence and seems in opposition to Russia's proposed Eurasian Economic Unit (EEU). Russia is a major source of fuel for China. The EEU now currently seems to be wrapped within BRI – an indication of weakness (Dragneva and Wolczuk 2017). Russia may also be looking to China for investment in Russia and its contiguous zones. Russia and China, particularly acting in unison, may be threats to any (illegal) assertion of US dominance over the planet. But they are not threats to the USA as such.

Notwithstanding considerations of Russia's weakness relative to the west in all but nuclear strength, NATO has continued to act in preparation for war. In June 2018, for example, defense ministers of all NATO member states decided to take all necessary steps over the following two years to be able to mobilize a total of 90 military, naval, and air force combat units at short notice and at any time (Link 2018).

The nuclear question

Putin is not Yeltsin, and the west was underprepared for Putin even though Putin was Yeltsin's choice as successor. Putin was a capitalist, but a nationalist capitalist, whose conservation of control of powerful oil and gas companies in Russian hands helped seed the new western hostility to his regime together with persistent western claims of its "corruption" on account of the fact that Russia has kept the western energy companies at bay (Mercouris 2014). In terms of Russia's ability to sustain and to modernize a nuclear threat, however, the answer is yes, Russia is an obstacle to western regional aspirations, perhaps much more than the west appears to appreciate. Nuclear war remains a very real threat to the planet, probably the second most likely cause of the disappearance of the human species after climate change. Whereas climate change is unlikely to have fatal consequences for the planet as a whole before the current century is complete, nuclear war can break out at any time. Escalation of hostile rhetoric between nuclear powers enhances the likelihood that such weapons will be used, whether accidentally – there have been several "near misses," subject to intense analysis among nuclear weapons experts both in the USA and Russia – or the result of strategic deployment. Endorsing concern about accidental triggers of nuclear war, President Trump in Helsinki in 2018 even criticized NATO's collective defense terms on the grounds that any small NATO member could quickly escalate the entire alliance into a world war by calling upon its nuclear partners to intervene (Ditz 2018b). The continuing threat of nuclear weapons has been underlined by Daniel Ellsberg in his book *The Doomsday Machine* (Ellsberg 2017). Once a believer and influential promoter of nuclear weapons as a means of deterrence, Ellsberg now says he was a collaborator in an "insane plan" for "retaliatory genocide." Ellsberg discovered many plausible scenarios in which officers might feel authorized to launch a nuclear attack in the absence of presidential orders. Safeguards were easy to circumvent.

Ellsberg writes of nuclear destruction:

> Here's the scenario: the fallout would remain mostly limited to the northern hemisphere but the smoke and soot generated by fierce firestorms in hundreds of burning cities would be lofted into the stratosphere, where it would not rain out and would remain for a decade or more, enveloping the globe in smoke and blocking out sunlight, lowering temperatures to the level of the last Ice Age, and killing all harvests worldwide, causing near-universal starvation within a year or two.
>
> (Ellsberg 2018).

The list of accompanying collapses includes these: impacts of the blasts; massive radioactive fallout; targeting of nuclear reactors that significantly increases fallout of long-lived isotopes; massive firestorms that burn urban areas of tens or hundreds of thousands of square miles/kilometers around hundreds of cities; 150 million tons of smoke rising into the stratosphere, quickly spreading around the world where it remains for many years to block and absorb sunlight; gigantic ground-hugging clouds of toxic smoke; enormous quantities of industrial chemicals entering the environment; smoke blocking up to 70% of the sunlight in the Northern Hemisphere, and up to 35% of the sunlight in the South; surface temperatures on Earth becoming as cold as they were 18,000 years ago at the height of the last Ice Age; average global precipitation falling by 45% due to the prolonged cold; growing seasons virtually eliminated for many years; massive destruction of the protective ozone layer, allowing intense levels of dangerous UV light to penetrate the atmosphere and reach the surface of the Earth. Already stressed land and marine ecosystems would collapse. Unable to grow food, most humans would starve to death. A mass extinction event would occur (Glikson 2018).

The numbers of nuclear missiles have declined considerably since Cold War peaks, but both the USA and Russia have worked on enhancing their lethality: the destructive power of US warheads is now much greater than it was (Kristensen et al 2017), while Russia claims to have reduced the size of warheads, to have developed warheads that can be carried by underwater drones, and to have hypersonic nuclear missiles (Kinzhal missile system) and hypersonic glide vehicles (Avangard) that can penetrate any missile defense system (Carroll 2018). To emphasize that final point: Vladimir Putin has for many years maintained that Russia now has the capability to overcome any US missile defense ("Star Wars") system – not so difficult, after all, considering that some critics of US missile defense policy such as MIT's Ted Postol have long maintained that the system does not work in any case (Tsuruoko 2018; Beckhusen 2013). It can easily be overcome by the firing of numerous decoys. Tests have often been designed to replicate conditions most favorable for interceptors to work, rather than to demonstrate the extent of the likelihood that in real-world conditions they can work at all. Russian missile expert Anrdei Martyanov, in a 2018 book, considered that the missile gap between the US and Russia, in favor of Russia, had become "a technological abyss," with ballistic missiles "capable of trajectories which render any kind of anti-ballistic defense useless." Star Wars and its derivatives were now "obsolete." Until recently, in any case, mismatching sophistication of early warning systems (that favor the US because they are satellite rather than land-based) enhanced the possibility of error and of poor judgment given the reduced time of warning available to the Russians, a problem that was intensified by removal of "buffer zones" between NATO members and the Russian Federation.

Given the numbers and power of the missiles at their disposal (90% of the global total), it is very likely that a conflict between the USA and Russia would indeed lead to the end of the world so far as human beings are concerned. China too must be factored into the equation since it is a nuclear power, with significant investment in technological advance of its nuclear capacity (including the Starry Sky-2 hypersonic missile successfully tested in 2018 [Zhen 2018]). A more limited conflict between, say, India and Pakistan (entirely thinkable, given the mismatch of populations between the two countries, Pakistan's greater sense of threat, and the gathering conflicts over water that will be exacerbated by climate change) may not wipe out the human species but would certainly wipe out a good proportion of it. The notion that armies can deploy lower-power nuclear weapons in more "surgical" fashion is the height of foolishness since the dispatch of any such weapon may well provoke a response that "ups the ante."

In 2002 the George W. Bush administration unilaterally withdrew from the 1972 Anti-Ballistic Missile (ABM) Treaty, on its expiry, on the grounds that it had become an obstacle to building a national missile defense. The ABM Treaty had barred both superpowers from deploying national defenses against long-range ballistic missiles and from building the foundations for such a defense. The treaty had allowed both sides to build defenses against short- and medium-range ballistic missiles.

There may have been valid reasons why this treaty needed overhaul, but unilateral withdrawal signaled a staggering arrogance and disdain for Russia, and conformed to the "Bush Doctrine," as outlined in the National Security Strategy of the United States in 2002, of US dominance over any actual or potential threat to its power.

A new START (Strategic Arms Reduction Treaty) treaty – START 2 – was signed between both countries in 1993 (replacing the first START treaty of 1991. It never came into effect. Russia withdrew in 2002 after the USA had abandoned the ABM treaty. START 2 was replaced by SORT (Strategic Offensive Reductions Treaty). In SORT both parties agreed to limit their nuclear arsenal to between 1,700 and 2,200 operationally deployed warheads each. It was replaced by NEW START in 2012, due to expire in 2021 – with the possibility of a five-year extension, even though some voices in Washington have urged non-renewal. NEW START committed both parties to a cap by 2018 of 1,550 deployed, strategic nuclear warheads and bombs, 700 ICBM and SLBM and nuclear bombers, and 800 deployed and non-deployed ICBM, SLBM, and bombers.

Walking away from the ABM Treaty in 2002, the USA in effect conveyed the message to Russia that Russia needed to upgrade its nuclear weapons. Both Russia and the USA have developed relatively low-power nuke warheads deliverable from air or sea. Putin in 2018 has unveiled several new strategic weapons designed to nullify any missile defense shield the United States has deployed, is currently deploying, or will seek to deploy in the next 10 to 15 years.

Early in 2018 the USA had 4,000 nuclear warheads for delivery by more than 800 ballistic missiles and aircraft. Of the 4,000, 1,800 were deployed, of which 150 were based in Europe. Some land-based nukes were on high alert. The other weapons were in storage. Another 2,350 were "retired" and waiting for reconstruction. Russia had 4,350 nuclear warheads, of which 1,600 were structured, strategic, deployed weapons, 920 strategic weapons were in storage, and 1,500 were non-strategic; 2,500 were in retirement, awaiting dismantlement (Richman 2018).

In 2007, Russia leaked details about the RS-28 "Sarmat" heavy missile, a direct descendant of the R-36 heavy ballistic missile (Ritter 2018b). The R-36's large throw-weight (almost 20,000 pounds) allowed it to carry either a single extremely large warhead of 20 megatons or 10 independently targetable warheads of 500 to 750 kilotons. The START I Treaty had seen the number of R-36 missiles deployed reduced from 308 to 154, and the entire R-36 arsenal was scheduled to be eliminated under the terms of the START II Treaty. After Russia withdrew from START II Treaty it maintained its fleet of R-36 missiles. Russia then embarked on an expensive service life extension program to keep the R-36 operationally viable through 2020 and continued work on its replacement, the R-28. In identifying some of the strategic advantages, Ritter noted among other things that the R-28 ("Sarmat") provided Russia with the "means to avoid launch detection, evade all missile defense systems, and destroy America's land-based intercontinental ballistic missile (ICBM) nuclear force," giving Russia a "genuine first-strike capability that nullifies one third of America's nuclear triad" (Ritter 2018b).

Among recent Russian advances is its nuclear-powered autonomous torpedo, the Poseidon unmanned underwater vehicle (UUV), originally known as "Status-6." On March 1, 2018, Putin officially confirmed the weapon's existence, noting that Russia had developed unmanned submersible vehicles that can move at extreme depths, intercontinentally, at a speed multiple times higher than the speed of submarines, cutting-edge torpedoes, and all kinds of surface vessels (RT 2018b). Its main goal is

> to deliver a thermonuclear warhead to enemy shores in order to destroy important coastal infrastructure and industrial objects, as well as ensure massive damage to the enemy's territory by subjecting vast areas to radioactive tsunamis and other devastating consequences of a nuclear explosion.
>
> (ibid)

From the Obama Administration, Donald Trump had inherited a plan to refurbish the US nuclear force at an estimated cost of $1 trillion over three decades, and which would include the development of submarine-based cruise and ballistic missiles. Trump's "America First" National Security Strategy of December 2017 and Nuclear Posture Review of February 2018 threatened to push the total cost to $2 trillion. These measures would also reduce the threshold for nuclear engagement so that the USA could use nuclear weapons in response to non-nuclear attacks, even to cyberattacks on civilian populations or infrastructure (Wittner 2018).

The reckless abandonment by the Bush administration of the ABM treaty was exacerbated in 2018 by the Trump administration's treat to withdraw from the Intermediate-Range Nuclear Forces (INF) treaty, first signed by US President Reagan and Soviet President Gorbachev in 1987. It prohibited Washington and Moscow from developing short- and medium-range missiles and was regarded as a measure to reduce the likelihood of first strikes, since it limited nuclear weapons to ICBMs which provided each side with warning time. The pretext for the threat to walk away from INF was the alleged non-compliance by Russia. The treaty had reduced the necessity for land-based nuclear missiles. Possibly the abandonment of the INF treaty was a response to Russian deployment of the land-based, intermediate-range

SSC-8 cruise missile which in turn had been prompted by US deployment on the borders of Russia of Star Wars defense missiles systems (which can easily be converted to offensive). The real objective would likely be the freedom it would give to locate missiles in locations better suited for containment of China (Damon 2018c). In response both China and Russia have intensified their warnings to domestic and foreign audiences of their need to prepare for war (The Saker 2018). Vladimir Putin declared in October 2018 that any withdrawal from the INF would see an "immediate and mirror-like" response from Moscow.

The unending stream of western anti-Russian propaganda

Anti-Russian propaganda has continued in western media since the collapse of the Soviet Union. Significant examples in the period of RussiaGate have included western representations of Russian activity in Ukraine and in Syria. An example of "atrocity propaganda" for the purposes of stoking further conflict was western and Ukrainian manufacture of the "Russia shot down civilian airliner MH17" narrative, with reference to the tragedy that befell a civilian Malaysian airways flight over eastern Ukraine in 2014. Western media largely failed to put this in a context of reference to many previous, comparable, and possibly accidental, western attacks on civilian aircraft over conflict zones, as in the case of the US shooting down over the Persian Gulf of Iran Air Flight 655 which was *en route* from Tehran to Dubai in 1988. Western condemnation of Russia, unassisted by US surveillance data which remained suspiciously elusive, and as reflected in the Dutch Investigation Team reports of 2015, 2016, and 2018, was deeply problematic (Boyd-Barrett 2017, 2018; Van de Pijl 2018; O'Neill 2018b). Among other things, the investigation did the following:

1   Incorporated to an unusual degree the social media findings of a supposedly private investigative agency, Bellingcat.com that has since evolved into an outlet for the aggressively pro-NATO think tank, Atlantic Council.
2   With the backing of substantial western media insistence but little logic, the investigation presumed from the outset that Russia was the culprit and therefore debarred Russia from being a member of the investigative team; Belgium, which had lost no citizens, was included in the investigation team, possibly because Brussels is the headquarters of NATO.
3   With the backing of substantial western media insistence but little logic, the investigation from the outset regarded Ukraine as victim and included the Kiev regime as a member of the investigative team, even

though there has always been substantial reason (e.g. Ukrainian ownership of many Russian-made BUK missile-launchers, parked in the Donbass) to regard the Kiev regime as a leading suspect, with stronger motive than Russia – since the demonization of Russia could only assist its cause.

4   The investigation played down Ukrainian culpability, in that Ukraine continued to permit the passage of civilian airliners over contested territories, territories in which numerous BUKs were stationed and over which many military aircraft had already been shot down. When the Dutch investigation team reported in May 2018, it released identification details of the BUK missile for the first time, enabling Russia to supply evidence that the missile launcher in question had been transferred to Ukraine in 1986 and never returned. The Russians attributed the attack to a Ukrainian unit under an identified command which had been radar tracking MH17 the day of the shooting (undermining Ukraine's always implausible claim that radar systems had been under maintenance).

5   The investigation team worked closely and in friendly collaboration with Ukrainian intelligence (SBU) in Kiev. Less than an hour after the shooting down, it was the SBU who removed air traffic control tapes, never to be seen again. Although the USA consistently accused Russia, it never released its own satellite data for public scrutiny.

6   The terms of the investigation, signed in secret in August 2014, permitted the member nations to veto publication of any evidence of which they disapproved. Long before conclusions were published, member nations, particularly Ukraine and Australia, had denounced Russia as culprit.

Equally relevant in this context was Russia's adept diplomacy in 2013 when it salvaged western embarrassment over the failure of US and UK governments to secure popular support for a western invasion of Syria on the disputed pretext that the Baa'thist and socialist regime of Bashar al-Assad had used chemical weapons against jihadist rebels in East Ghouta that year (the East Ghouta incident is described at length in Boyd-Barrett 2015). As a compromise measure, Russia successfully proposed that the OPCW should organize the collection and destruction of all of the Syrian regime's stocks of chemical weapons. Russia's subsequent military intervention provided an effective counter-thrust to the gains of ISIS, exposing US lack of seriousness and its duplicitous western support for al Qaeda–linked jihadist groups. In the meantime, accusations against the Syrian government for alleged use of chemical weapons – their removal from Assad's stockpiles notwithstanding (OPCW claimed a success rate of detection of well over 90%) – were regularly resurrected by jihadists and their western and other sponsors, with little or no critical mainstream media coverage even while evidence mounted of the use of chemical weapons by jihadist groups for the purposes of staging false flag incidents as leverage to legitimate western support for the "rebels" (Strack 2017; Mackie 2017; Doornbos and Moussa 2016; McKeigue, Larson et al. 2018).

A full assessment of the Russian intervention in Syria 2015–2018 observed this:

> The US, Israel, Turkey, Saudi Arabia, Qatar and other countries of the so-called civilized world were either providing direct and indirect supplies or assistance to Jabhat al-Nusra and its allies in an effort to overthrow the Assad government. The US-led coalition against ISIS achieved little success in combating the terrorist group and destroying its infrastructure. The so-called Caliphate had clearly expanded its territory and power since the coalition's formal establishment on June 13, 2014. ISIS' oil business was on the rise with illegal oil flows streaming throughout the region and even reaching the broader international market.
>
> (Southfront 2018)

In the case of the chemical attack reported to have taken place in Dhouma early in April 2018, subsequent evidence suggests there may have been no such attack at all, but possibly a conventional Syrian air force attack as Syria regained territory occupied by ISIS (Fisk 2018). As on many previous occasions of such allegations that have later been debunked or the evidence found seriously wanting, the US and its allies, and western mainstream media, leaped to the conclusion that the Syrian Arab Army, answerable to the Assad regime in Damascus, and with every possible motive for avoiding the use of chemical weapons, was responsible. It was alleged that traces of both chlorine and sarin had been found. Investigative journalist Seymour Hersh cited 1950s US research showing that nerve agents mixed with chlorine would immediately be chlorinated and therefore ineffective [RT 2018a; see also Hersh 1968]; Whitaker 2018). Amidst combined accusations against the Syrian Arab Army from jihadist groups, a *New York Times* investigation in support of these claims (Brown et al 2018) – based not on a visit to the site but on a simulated model of it – and a US "retaliatory" military strike, little attention was given to a report from veteran foreign correspondent Robert Fisk, and confirmed by a US television news organization ((Syrmopoulos 2018b) that found no evidence of chemical weapons. The OPCW interim report on the Dhouma incident published on July 6, 2018, was compiled from on-site visits, witness interviews, and data collection. It found no evidence of the use of nerve agents (OPCW 2018). This did not stop some media, including the BBC, from claiming, falsely, that the OPCW *had* found evidence of a chemical weapons attack (for a fuller account of the Dhouma incident, see Boyd-Barrett 2019b).

Evidence from the final OPCW report, and a subsequently leaked technical assessment April/May 2019 suggests that evidence of a chlorine bomb attack was staged (McKeigue, Miller and Robinson 2019).

Conclusion

In the Introduction, I acknowledged considerable sympathy in Russia for at least some western mainstream media, a phenomenon that links to a pro-western "Atlanticist" movement nurtured by the USA. A significant proportion of Russian intelligentsia is pro-western, and critical of the Putin regime and its system of "managed democracy." This puts the Putin regime at a disadvantage: if Russian intelligentsia lacks a critical appreciation of western and in particular NATO *realpolitik*, this may further encourage regime-change maneuvers by western powers.

I have talked about the competitive struggle for influence over EurAsia between the USA, Western Europe, Russia, and China. This has considerable implications for the potential chances for an enduring BRICS alliance, China's One Belt, One Road initiative, and the Chinese-sponsored Asian Infrastructure Investment Bank. At present the BRICS alliance comprises countries that are split between western and eastern orientations, separated by language and culture, possessing different national interests and contrasting stages of economic development. Chinese growth in itself, however, is a much more substantial phenomenon. I have considered the role of Russia as an independent source of energy and energy wealth, with implications for the opportunities that remain for western oil and gas companies in EurAsia, the supply of energy to Europe and China, and the influence of Russia as ally in the Middle East to Syria and Iran. It is in EurAsia that we see the sharpening tensions between two great power blocs: the USA, in an increasingly wobbly alliance with the European Union, and China in cautious alliance with Russia. US competitive rhetoric has focused primarily on Russia for almost 20 years in a mounting crescendo of angst, even as the trade wars ignited by President Trump in 2018 mainly had to do with China.

The stream of western propaganda invective against Russia should be taken less on its own terms and more in relation to this broader context in which Russia under a different regime could be a valuable ally and source of wealth for the west, or in which Russia in alliance with China could become an existential threat to western interests. In exploring such propaganda I have examined the events in Dhouma in 2018 and the allegations of use of chemical weapons as yet one further likely example of "fake news" alongside the re-ignition of claims that Russia's ally, Iran, constitutes a "nuclear" threat, deserving of sanctions; claims that Russia was responsible for the assassination attempt on Sergei and Julia Skripal in the UK and therefore deserving of sanctions, or worse; and continuing claims that Russia was the aggressor nation in the Ukraine conflict. All these examples operate to heighten or escalate a rhetoric of hostility that contributes to the threat of nuclear Armageddon.

The rhetoric is further enflamed by obfuscations, exaggerations, and outright lies and deceptions concerning the alleged role of Russia in "subverting US democracy" by means of actions that allegedly favored the electoral chances of Donald Trump in 2016. These allegations mostly had to do with claims of Russian manipulation of voter perceptions and beliefs through social media; the uses of "bots," "trolls," and deceptive advertising; and claims that Russian intelligence services hacked the emails of Hillary Clinton, the Democratic National Campaign and its chairman, John Podesta, and handed these to WikiLeaks for publication; also that senior Russian politicians and business figures colluded with members of the Trump Campaign to favor Trump. Very little is proven beyond doubt and much may be based on lies and fabrications. Much of it points to deep levels of insecurity about the role of corporatized social media such as Facebook, Google, and Twitter who likely failed to protect the interests of their users to the standard that users imagined and to which they were entitled. Notwithstanding egregious shortcomings on the part of social media, the political reaction to Russia-Gate has been such as to feed the self-importance of their executives, granting them ever more over-weaning, undemocratic, and unaccountable power in determining what contents their users should be able to access, which sources of information should be foregrounded, which should be marginalized or excluded altogether – in other words, the power to shape and construct the information environment on which users depend to make sense of their world. This has occurred at precisely the same time that the US FCC has threatened to abandon its previous undertakings to "net neutrality," ushering in an era of information control in which the strongest information monopolies can select, emphasize, increase, or decrease accessibility to information (by means of price, quality, or speed of delivery mechanisms) at whim.

The broader question still is about "fake news" and its contribution to a "post-truth era," and I conclude that this issue can only be dealt with satisfactorily by means of a frank assessment of the limitations of those public media that must operate within the constraints of deeply unequal power structures, whether in the domains of political or corporate power, and by means of an assessment of how this situation, in turn, relates to phenomena of imperialism and neo-imperialism and the manifold ways in which mainstream media (legacy and online) are active players in the construction of the information environments that underwrite ideological justifications for such phenomena.

References

ABC News (2018, March 16) Cambridge Analytica bosses claimed they invented 'Crooked Hillary' campaign, won Donald Trump the presidency. *ABC News/AFP*. Available online at www.abc.net.au/news/2018-03-21/cambridge-analytica-claimed-it-secured-donald-trump-presidentia/9570690.

Agence France Presse (2018, April 14) Salisbury attack: Russia claims chemical weapons watchdog manipulated findings. *The Guardian*. Available online at www.theguardian.com/uk-news/2018/apr/15/salisbury-attack-russia-claims-chemical-weapons-watchdog-manipulated-findings.

Ahmed, N. (2017, December 29) Facebook will become more powerful than the NSA in less than 10 years – unless we stop it. *Insurge Intelligence*. Available online at https://medium.com/insurge-intelligence/how-facebook-will-infiltrate-national-elections-and-rule-the-world-in-less-than-10-years-unless-732da197b8fd

Ahmed, N. (2018a, March 7) Army document: US strategy to 'dethrone' Putin for oil pipelines might provoke WW3. *Insurge Intelligence*. Available online at https://medium.com/insurge-intelligence/army-study-us-strategy-to-dethrone-putin-for-oil-pipelines-might-provoke-ww3-9b1d9dbe6be9.

Ahmed, N. (2018b, March 21) UK govt asked Cambridge Analytica Trump team for advice on "data in foreign policy." *Insurge Intelligence*. Available online at https://medium.com/insurge-intelligence/uk-govt-asked-cambridge-analytica-trump-team-for-advice-on-data-in-foreign-policy-aa046a9dd295

Al Jazeera (2018) The Lobby. *Al Jazeera English*. Available online at www.aljazeera.com/investigations/thelobby.

Aleem, Z. (2018, March 28) George Nader, one of the Trump-Russia investigation's most mysterious figures, explained. *Vox*. Available online at www.vox.com/policy-and-politics/2018/3/28/17165410/george-nader-trump-mueller-immunity-russia.

Almukhtar, S. (2018, April 13) Most chemical attacks in Syria get little attention. Here are 34 confirmed cases. *The New York Times*. Available online at www.nytimes.com/interactive/2018/04/13/world/middleeast/syria-chemical-attacks-maps-history.html.

Ambroz, J. (2018, May 22) Dark money groups are funding two out of every three TV ads in congressional races. *Alternet.org*. Available online at www.alternet.org/dark-money-groups-are-funding-two-out-every-three-tv-ads-congressional-races.

Amer, K and Noujaim, J. (2019) (Directors). *The great hack*. Available online at www.imdb.com/title/tt9358204/

Anderlini, J. (2018, August 8) China and Russia's dangerous liaison. *Financial Times*. Available online at www.ft.com/content/1b4e6d78-9973-11e8-9702-5946bae 86e6d.

Anderson, B. and Horvath, B. (2017, September 2) The rise of the weaponized AI propaganda machine. *Scout*. Available online at https://scout.ai/story/the-rise-of-the-weaponized-ai-propaganda-machine.

Associated Press (2017, June 1) The Latest: France says no trace of Russian hacking Macron. *APNews.com*. Available online at www.apnews.com/fc570e4b400 f4c7db3b0d739e9dc5d4d.

Associated Press (2018a, March 7) Facebook says accounts from Russia spent $100,000 on ads during the 2016 election. *Los Angeles Times*. Available online at www.latimes.com/politics/washington/la-na-essential-washington-updates-facebook-says-accounts-from-russia-1504779562-htmlstory.html.

Associated Press (2018b, May 3) Czech president: Czechs made Novichok, citing spy agency. *APNews.com*. Available online at www.apnews.com/08f7a9ff33294 87e8dcb88e62a2111ba.

Auletta, K. (2018) *Frenemies: The epic disruption of the ad business (and everything else)*. New York: Penguin/Random House.

Bamford, J. (2019, February 11) The spy who wasn't. *The New Republic*. Available online at https://newrepublic.com/article/153036/maria-butina-profile-wasnt-russian-spy

Barrett, D. and Hamburger, T. (2018, January 10) Feud over Trump dossier intensifies with release of interview transcript. *Washington Post*. Available online at www.washingtonpost.com/world/national-security/feinstein-releases-testimony-of-glenn-simpson-whose-research-firm-fusion-gps-was-behind-trump-dossier/2018/01/09/15da150a-f562-11e7-beb6-c8d48830c54d_story.html?noredirect=on&utm_term=.0c79f6a6c102.

Bartlett, E. (2018, April 15) Caught in a lie, US & allies bomb Syria the night before international inspectors arrive. *RT.com*. Available online at www.rt.com/op-ed/424186-us-allies-syria-lie.

BBC (2016, January 21) Litvinenko inquiry: Key findings. *BBC*. Available online at www.bbc.com/news/uk-35371344.

BBC One – Panorama (2018, November 22) Salisbury nerve agent attack – The inside story. London: *British Broadcasting Corporation*.

Beam, M., Hutchens, M. and J. Hmielowski (2017) Facebook news and (de)polarization: Reinforcing spirals in the 2016 US election. *Information, Communication & Society*, 21:7, 940–958, DOI: 10.1080/1369118X.2018.1444783.

Beckhusen, R. (2013, July 9) Your $170 billion missile defenses don't work. *Medium.com*. Available online at https://medium.com/war-is-boring/your-170-billion-missile-defenses-dont-work-51fa276a7983

Beeley, V. (2018, July 2) False flag fail: How Syrian civilians derailed White Helmet 'chemical' stunt in Eastern Ghouta. *21st Century Wire*. Available online at https://21stcenturywire.com/2018/07/02/false-flag-fail-how-syrian-civilians-derailed-white-helmets-chemical-stunt-in-eastern-ghouta.

Benjamin, M. (2016) *Behind the U.S.-Saudi connection.* New York: OR books.

Benkler, Y., Faris, R. and H. Roberts (2018) *Network propaganda. Manipulation, disinformation, and radicalization in American politics.* London and New York: Oxford University Press

Benkler, Y., Faris R., Roberts, H. and E. Zuckerman (2018) Study: Breitbart-led right-wing media ecosystem altered broader media agenda. *Columbia Journalism Review.* Available online at www.cjr.org/analysis/breitbart-media-trump-harvard-study.php.

Bennis, P. (2015) *Understanding ISIS and the new global war on terror. A primer.* Northampton, MA: Olive Branch Press.

Bensinger, K., Elder, M. and M. Schoofs (2017, January 11) These reports allege Trump has deep ties to Russia. *Buzzfeed.com.* Available online at www.buzz feed.com/kenbensinger/these-reports-allege-trump-has-deep-ties-to-russia?utm_ term=.arkj044aE#.mrPV3yymv.

Bergman, R. (2018) *Rise and kill first: The secret history of Israel's targeted assassinations.* London: John Murray.

Berman, R. (2016, October 12) What the WikiLeaks emails say about Clinton. *The Atlantic.* Available online at www.theatlantic.com/politics/archive/2016/10/wikileaks-clinton-emails-podesta-sanders-trump/503711.

Biersack, B. (2018, February 7) 8 years later: How Citizens United changed campaign finance. *OpenSecrets.org.* Available online at www.opensecrets.org/news/2018/02/how-citizens-united-changed-campaign-finance.

Birnbaum, M. (2018, March 27) Here are all the countries that just expelled Russian diplomats. *The Washington Post.* Available online at www.washingtonpost.com.

Blake, A. (2018) Is floating a $50 million Trump Tower penthouse for Vladimir Putin illegal? *Washington Post.* Available online at www.washingtonpost.com/politics/2018/11/30/is-floating-million-trump-tower-penthouse-vladimir-putin-illegal/?utm_term=.ed3b420f7961.

Bloomberg News (2018, February 16) Russia spent $1.25M per month on ads, acted like an ad agency: Mueller. *AdAge.* Available online at http://adage.com/article/digital/russia-spent-1-25m-ads-acted-agency-mueller/312424

Blum, W. (2004) *Killing hope: U.S. military and CIA interventions since World War II.* Revised edition. Monroe, ME: Common Courage Press.

Blumenthal, M. (2016, October 2) How the White Helmets became international heroes while pushing U.S. military intervention and regime change in Syria. *Alternet.org.* Available online at www.alternet.org/grayzone-project/how-white-helmets-became-international-heroes-while-pushing-us-military.

Borger, J. (2017, July 1) Cyber expert says GOP operative wanted to expose hacked Clinton emails. *The Guardian.* Available online at www.theguardian.com/us-news/2017/jul/01/hillary-clinton-hacked-emails-russia-trump-peter-smith-matt-tait.

Boyd-Barrett, O. (2015) *Media imperialism.* London: Sage

Boyd-Barrett, O. (2017) *Western mainstream media and the Ukraine crisis. A case-study in conflict propaganda.* London: Routledge.

Boyd-Barrett, O. (2018) MH17 as free-floating atrocity propaganda. In S. Coban (ed.) *Media, ideology and hegemony. Critical social science,* vol. 122. Leiden, Netherlands: Brill.

Boyd-Barrett, O. (2019a) The Great Game for EurAsia and the Skripal affair. In O. Boyd-Barrett and T. Mirrlees (eds.) *Media imperialism: Continuity and change*. Boulder, CO: Rowman and Littlefield.

Boyd-Barrett, O. (2019b) Western news media, propaganda and pretexts for neoliberal war. In O. Boyd-Barrett and T. Mirrlees (eds.) *Media imperialism: Continuity and change*. Boulder, CO: Rowman and Littlefield.

Brennan, D. (2018, May 2) Why is Russia cutting military spending? *Newsweek*. Available online at www.newsweek.com/why-russia-cutting-military-spending-908069.

Brian, M. (2011, May 2) Wikileaks founder: Facebook is the most appalling spy machine that has ever been invented. *Thenextweb.com*. Available online at https://thenextweb.com/facebook/2011/05/02/wikileaks-founder-facebook-is-the-most-appalling-spy-machine-that-has-ever-been-invented/

Brown, E. (2018, May 10) Mueller indicted Concord Catering for conspiring in the 2016 U.S. Election. But Its lawyer says the company didn't exist then. *Reason.com*. Available online at https://reason.com/blog/2018/05/10/mueller-indicted-a-ham-sandwich

Brown, M., Koettl, C., Reneau, N., Singhvi, A., Marcolini, B., Al-Hlou, Y. and D. Jordan (2018, June 25) How Bashar Al-Assad gassed Syrian civilians. *New York Times*. Available online at www.nytimes.com/video/world/middleeast/100000005840873/syria-chlorine-bomb-assad.html?emc=edit_th_180626&nl=todaysheadlines&nlid=529785730626.

Brownstein, R. (2016, November 10) How the Rustbelt paved Trump's road to victory. *The Atlantic*. Available online at www.theatlantic.com/politics/archive/2016/11/trumps-road-to-victory/507203.

Bump, P. (2018, March 19) Everything you need to know about the Cambridge Analytica-Facebook debacle. *The Washington Post*. Available online at www.washingtonpost.com.

Buncomb, A. (2018, July 31) Israeli intervention in US elections 'vastly overwhelms' anything Russia has done, claims Noam Chomsky. *The Independent*. Available online at www.independent.co.uk/news/world/americas/us-politics/israel-us-elections-intervention-russia-noam-chomsky-donald-trump-a8470481.html.

Burgess, M. (2017, December 13) Facebook claims Russia paid for 3 ads around Brexit – costing 73p. *Wired.com*. Available online at www.wired.co.uk/article/russia-brexit-parliamentary-inquiry-damian-collins.

Burnett, S. (2018, August 5) Twitter's 'bot' push sweeps up others. *Associated Press*, reprinted in Ventura County Star, 1.

Buyniski, H. (2018 July 15) FBI chief Mueller drops indictments against Russia intel Ops. as Deep State panics over Trump-Putin summit. *Global Research*. Available online at https://williambowles.info/2018/07/16/fbi-chief-mueller-drops-indictments-against-russia-intel-ops-as-deep-state-panics-over-trump-putin-summit-by-helen-buyniski/

Byers, D. (2017, October 31) Facebook estimates 126 million people were served content from Russia-linked pages. *Money CNN.com*. Available online at http://money.cnn.com/2017/10/30/media/russia-facebook-126-million-users/index.html.

Cadwalladr, C. (2017, February 25) Revealed: How US billionaire helped to back Brexit. *The Guardian*. Available online at www.theguardian.com/politics/2017/feb/26/us-billionaire-mercer-helped-back-brexit.

Cadwalladr, C. (2018, March 18) 'I made Steve Bannon's psychological warfare tool': Meet the data war whistleblower. *The Guardian*. Available online at www.theguardian.com/news/2018/mar/17/data-war-whistleblower-christopher-wylie-faceook-nix-bannon-trump.

Cadwalladr, C. and Graham-Harrison, E. (2018, March 17) Cambridge Analytica: Links to Moscow oil firm and St Petersburg university. *The Guardian*. Available online at www.theguardian.com/news/2018/mar/17/cambridge-academic-trawling-facebook-had-links-to-russian-university.

Carroll, O. (2018, March 1) Russia has 'unstoppable' supersonic nuclear missile that cannot be traced by Western defence systems, says Putin. *The Independent*. Available online at www.independent.co.uk/news/world/europe/russia-nuclear-weapon-tests-drones-west-nato-defence-systems-putin-presidential-address-a82342 96.html.

Cartalucci, T. (2013, April 12) Exposed: Syrian Observatory for Human Rights is EU-funded fraud. *Information Clearing House*. Available online at www.infor mationclearinghouse.info/article34582.htm.

Cartalucci, T. (2018, June 17) Atlantic Council lies dashed "on the rocks" in Syria. *Global Research*. Available at www.globalresearch.ca/atlantic-council-lies-dashed-on-the-rocks-in-syria/5644450.

Cebul, D. (2018, May 2) US remains top military spender, SIPRI reports. *Defense news.com*. Available online at www.defensenews.com/industry/2018/05/02/us-remains-top-military-spender-sipri-reports.

Chalfant, M. (2019, January 13) Manafort developments trigger new 'collusion' debate. The Hill. Available online at https://thehill.com/policy/national-security/424986-manafort-developments-trigger-new-collusion-debate.

Channel 4 News (2018, March 19) Cambridge Analytica uncovered: Secret filming reveals election tricks. *Channel 4*. Available online at www.youtube.com/watch?v=mpbeOCKZFfQ.

Chapman, P. (2009) *Bananas. How the United Fruit Company shaped the world*. Edinburgh, UK: Canongate.

Chen, A. (2018, February 16) What Mueller's indictment reveals about Russia's IRA. *The New Yorker*. Available online at www.newyorker.com/news/news-desk/what-muellers-indictment-reveals-about-russias-internet-research-agency.

Cheney, K. (2018a, June 23) FBI hands House GOP thousands of documents on Russia probe. *Politico.com*. Available online at www.politico.com/story/2018/06/23/fbi-russia-probe-documents-nunes-gowdy-goodlatte-667181.

Cheney, K. (2018b, October 12) Papadopoulos to speak with House investigators. *Politico.com*. Available online at www.politico.com/story/2018/10/12/papadopoulos-house-investigators-898099.

CNN (2016, November 23) Exit polls. *CNN.org*. Available online at www.cnn.com/election/2016/results/exit-polls.

Cobb, J. (2018, October 29) Voter-Suppression Tactics in the Age of Trump. *The New Yorker*. Available online at www.newyorker.com/magazine/2018/10/29/voter-suppression-tactics-in-the-age-of-trump.

Cockburn, P. (2015) *The rise of the Islamic State. ISIS and the new SUNNI revolution.* New York: Verso.

Cohen, S. (2018, June 20) Russiagate's 'core narrative' has always lacked actual evidence. *The Nation.* Available online at www.thenation.com/article/russiagates-core-narrative-always-lacked-actual-evidence.

Coles, T.J. (2018, October 8) Fake news and weaponized bots: How algorithms inflate profiles, spread disinfo and disrupt democracy. *Counterpunch.* Available online at www.counterpunch.org/2018/10/08/fake-news-and-weaponized-bots-how-algorithms-inflate-profiles-spread-disinfo-and-disrupt-democracy/

Confessore, N. and Dance, G. (2018, February 20) On social media, lax enforcement lets impostor accounts thrive. *New York Times.* Available online at www.nytimes.com/2018/02/20/technology/social-media-impostor-accounts.html.

Confessore, N., Dance, G., Harris, R. and M. Hansen (2018, January 20) The follower factory. *New York Times.* Available online at www.nytimes.com/interactive/2018/01/27/technology/social-media-bots.html.

Costa, R., Leonnig, C. and S. Harris (2018, May 21) Who is Stefan A. Halper, the FBI source who assisted the Russia investigation? *Washington Post.* Available online at www.washingtonpost.com/politics/who-is-stefan-a-halper-the-fbi-source-who-assisted-the-russia-investigation/2018/05/21/22c46caa-5d42–11e8–9ee3–49d6d4814c4c_story.html?noredirect=on&utm_term=.f6474a8eb83b.

Couts, A. (2014, March 12) NSA pretended to be Facebook in its effort to infect 'millions' of computers. *Digitaltrends.com.* Available online at www.digitaltrends.com/web/nsa-pretended-facebook-spread-malware.

Cunningham, F. (2018a, May 10) The lasting power of legacy media. *The American Interest.* Available online at www.the-american-interest.com/2018/05/10/the-lasting-power-of-legacy-media.

Cunningham, F. (2018b, July 23) British assassination campaign targeting Russian exiles? *Strategic Culture Foundation.* Available online at www.strategic-culture.org/news/2018/07/20/british-assassination-campaign-targeting-russian-exiles.html.

Cunningham, F. (2018c, September 20) The Skripal affair – Another false flag in NATO litany to criminalize Russia. *Information Clearing House.* Available online at www.informationclearinghouse.info/50305.htm.

Curtis, M. (2003) *Web of deceit: Britain's real foreign policy: Britain's real role in the world.* London: Vintage.

Curtis, M. (2012) *Secret affairs. Britain's collusion with radical Islam.* London: Serpent's Tail.

Curtis, M. (2018) *Secret affairs: Britain's collusion with radical Islam.* London: Profile Books.

Damon, A. (2018a, August 3) Facebook censorship targets the left. *World Socialist Web Site.* Available online at www.wsws.org/en/articles/2018/08/03/pers-a02.html.

Damon, A. (2018b, October 13) Pages purged by Facebook were on blacklist promoted by Washington Post. *World Socialist Web Site.* Available online at www.wsws.org/en/articles/2018/10/13/cens-o13.html.

Damon, A. (2018c, October 24) US missile treaty withdrawal: "Prepare for nuclear war." *World Socialist Web Site.* Available online at www.wsws.org/en/articles/2018/10/24/pers-o24.html.

Damon, A. (2018d, December 18) The disinformation campaign behind the allegations of Russian "disinformation." *World Socialist Web Site*. Available online at www.wsws.org/en/articles/2018/12/18/pers-d18.html.

Damon, A. and Niemuth, N. (2017, July 27) New Google algorithm restricts access to left-wing, progressive web sites. *World Socialist Web Site*. Available online at www.wsws.org/en/articles/2017/07/27/goog-j27.html.

Dance, G., LaForgia, M. and N. Confessore (2018, December 18) As Facebook raised a privacy wall, it carved an opening for tech giants. *New York Times*. Available online at www.nytimes.com/2018/12/18/technology/facebook-privacy.html.

Darcy, O. (2017, December 6) CNN corrects story on email to Trumps about Wikileaks. *CNN.com*. Available online at http://money.cnn.com/2017/12/08/media/cnn-correction-email-story/index.html

Davidson, A. (2019, January 25) Robert Mueller got Roger Stone. *The New Yorker*. Available online at www.newyorker.com/news/swamp-chronicles/robert-mueller-got-roger-stone.

Davidson, C. (2016) *Shadow wars. The secret struggle for the Middle East*. London: Oneworld Publications Ltd.

Davies, N. (2009) *Flat earth news*. London: Random House.

Davis, S. (2018, May 21) E-mails show FBI brass discussed dossier briefing details with CNN. *The Federalist*. Available online at http://thefederalist.com/2018/05/21/breaking-e-mails-show-fbi-brass-discussed-dossier-briefing-details-cnn

Desilver, D. (2018, May 21) U.S. trails most developed countries in voter turnout. *Pew Research Center*. Available online at www.pewresearch.org/fact-tank/2018/05/21/u-s-voter-turnout-trails-most-developed-countries.

Devoe, P. (2018, March 13) There's less than meets the eye to Mueller's Russian-organized rallies. *National Review*. Available online at www.nationalreview.com/2018/03/mueller-investigation-indictments-russian-organized-rallies-not-influential.

Ditz, J. (2018a, February 28) Russian bots are a favored excuse, But an invented one. *Anti-war.com*. Available online at https://news.antiwar.com/2018/02/28/russian-bots-are-a-favored-excuse-but-an-invented-one

Ditz, J. (2018b July 18) Trump warns NATO collective defense could start World War 3. *Antiwar.com*. Available online at https://news.antiwar.com/2018/07/18/trump-warns-nato-collective-defense-could-start-world-war-3

Ditz, J. (2018c, November 2) Jeff Bezos puts the Pentagon on his Monopoly board. *The American Conservative*. Available online at www.theamericanconservative.com/articles/amazon-joins-the-military-to-further-its-dominance.

Ditz, J. (2018d, November 5) Whatever happened to the Russia-Gate scandal? *AntiWar.com*. Available online at https://original.antiwar.com/justin/2018/11/04/whatever-happened-to-the-russia-gate-scandal/?fbclid=IwAR1CnV8nUmvGAgmKtMiWD45OdWGFr7PPIG_lnSFo6s5BEbp9kzGXmVY-Na0

Doornbos, H. and Moussa, J. (2016) How the Islamic State seized a chemical weapons stockpile. *Foreignpolicy.com*. Available online at http://foreignpolicy.com/2016/08/17/how-the-islamic-state-seized-a-chemical-weapons-stockpile

Dowling, N. (2017, January 17) Is the Christopher Steele dossier fake news? *CNN.com*. Available online at www.cnn.com/2017/01/16/opinions/is-it-fake-news-dowling/index.html.

Dragneva, R. and Wolczuk, K. (2017, May) *The Eurasian Economic Unit. Deals, rules and the exercise of power*. London: Chatham House. Available online at www.chathamhouse.org/.../2017-05-02-eurasian-economic-union-dragneva-wolczuk.

Dubois (2018, August 3) Lafarge investigation exposes US-French collusion with ISIS in Syria. *World Socialist Web Site*. Available online at www.wsws.org/en/articles/2018/08/03/lafa-a03.html.

Durden, T. (2018a, June 5) Joining some dots on the Skripal case: Part 2 – Four "Invisible" Clues. *Zerohedge.com*. Available online at www.zerohedge.com/news/2018-06-04/joining-some-dots-skripal-case-part-2-four-invisible-clues.

Durden, T. (2018b, July 7) Twitter purges 70 million accounts in 2 months, equal to 20% of active users. *Zerohedge.com*. Available online at www.zerohedge.com/news/2018-07-06/twitter-purges-70-million-accounts-two-months-equal-20-monthly-active-users.

Durden, T. (2018c, July 16) Putin claims US intelligence agents funneled $400 million to Clinton campaign. *Zerohedge.com*. Available online at www.zerohedge.com/news/2018-07-16/putin-claims-us-intelligence-agents-funneled-400-million-clinton-campaign.

Durden, T. (2018d, August 8) A four person NATO-funded team advises Facebook on flagging 'Propaganda.' *Zerohedge.com*. Available online at www.zerohedge.com/news/2018-08-07/four-person-nato-funded-team-advises-facebook-flagging-propaganda.

Durden, T. (2018e, November 11) This wont end well: How Guccifer 2 planted "fake Russian fingerprints" on "hacked" DNC docs. *ZeroHedge.com*. Available online at www.zerohedge.com/news/2018-11-26/how-guccifer-2-planted-fake-russian-fingerprints-leaked-dnc-docs.

Durden, T. (2018f, November 25) MI6 scrambling to stop Trump from releasing classified documents in Russia probe. *ZeroHedge.com*. Available online at www.zerohedge.com/news/2018-11-23/mi6-scrambling-stop-trump-releasing-classified-docs-russia-probe.

DW (2017, July 3) Frankfurt used as remote hacking base for the CIA: WikiLeaks. *DW*. Available online at www.dw.com/en/frankfurt-used-as-remote-hacking-base-for-the-cia-wikileaks/a-37841830.

Dwoskin, E. and Romm, T. (2018a, November 15) Facebook says it removed a flood of hate speech, terrorist propaganda and fake accounts from its site. *The Washington Post*. Available online at www.washingtonpost.com/technology/2018/11/15/facebook-says-it-removed-flood-hate-speech-terrorist-propaganda-fake-accounts-its-site/?utm_term=.a036a60039c5.

Dwoskin, E. and Romm, T. (2018b, October 11) Facebook purged over 800 U.S. accounts and pages for pushing political spam. *The Washington Post*. Available online at www.washingtonpost.com/technology/2018/10/11/facebook-purged-over-accounts-pages-pushing-political-messages-profit/?utm_term=.eeceb96e87f3.

Dyer, J. (2018, March 29) Anti-Democracy. *Boulder Weekly*. Available online at www.boulderweekly.com/news/cambridge-analytica-oil-industry-fracking.

Edwards, J. (2011, July 11) Social media is a tool of the CIA. Seriously. *CBSNews*. Available online at www.cbsnews.com/news/social-media-is-a-tool-of-the-cia-seriously.

Eliason, G. (2018a, January 25) Untying PropOrNot: Who they are . . . and a Look at 2017's biggest fake news story. *Washingtonsblog*. Available online at http://washingtonsblog.com/2018/01/untying-propornot-look-2017s-biggest-fake-news-story.html.

Eliason, G. (2018b June 25) Who is Fancy Bear and who are they working for? *Off-Guardian*. Available online at https://off-guardian.org/2018/06/25/who-is-fancy-bear-and-who-are-they-working-for/

Ellsberg, D. (2017) *The doomsday machine: Confessions of a nuclear war planner*. London: Bloomsbury.

Ellsberg, D. (2018) Omnicide. *Harper's Magazine*. Available online at https://harpers.org/blog/2017/12/omnicide.

European Union (2018, February 15) *Social media companies need to do more to fully comply with EU consumer rules*. Brussels: European Commission. Available online at http://europa.eu/rapid/press-release_IP-18-761_en.htm.

Ewing, P. (2018, April 25) What you need to know about The Russia investigations: The Dossier. *NPR*. Available online at www.npr.org/2018/04/25/586040491/what-you-need-to-know-about-the-russia-investigations-the-dossier.

Federal Bureau of Investigation (2016, July 5) *Statement by FBI Director James B. Comey on the Investigation of Secretary Hillary Clinton's Use of a Personal E-Mail System*. Washington D.C.: FBI National Press Office. Available online at www.fbi.gov/news/pressrel/press-releases/statement-by-fbi-director-james-b-comey-on-the-investigation-of-secretary-hillary-clinton2019s-use-of-a-personal-e-mail-system.

Feldman, B. (2017, October 20) Did Russia's Facebook ads actually swing the election? *New York Magazine*. Available online at http://nymag.com/selectall/2017/10/did-russias-facebook-ads-actually-swing-the-election.html.

Ferguson, S., McGregor, J. and J. Stevens (2017, October 17) Hillary Clinton says Julian Assange colluded with Russia to help Donald Trump win US election. *ABC News*. Available online at www.abc.net.au/news/2017-10-16/hillary-clinton-says-julian-assange-helped-donald-trump-win/9047944.

Fielding, N. and Cobain, I. (2011, March 17) Revealed: US spy operation that manipulates social media. *The Guardian*. Available online at www.theguardian.com/technology/2011/mar/17/us-spy-operation-social-networks.

Fisher, M. and Taub, A. (2018, April 25) How everyday social media users become real-world extremists. *The New York Times*. Available online at www.nytimes.com/2018/04/25/world/asia/facebook-extremism.html.

Fisk, R. (2018, April 17) The search for truth in the rubble of Douma – and one doctor's doubts over the chemical attack. *The Independent*. Available online at www.independent.co.uk/voices/syria-chemical-attack-gas-douma-robert-fisk-ghouta-damascus-a8307726.html.

Ford, P. (2018, July 2) Statement by Peter Ford, British Ambassador to Syria, 2003–6, Representative of the Commissioner General of UNRWA, 2006–14. *Syria in Perspective: 38th Human Rights Council*: Side event organized by the International Association of Democratic Lawyers, Geneva 27 June 2018. Patreon.com. Available online at www.patreon.com/posts/exclusive-peter-19837790?utm_medium=social&utm_source=twitter&utm_campaign=postshare.

Frier, S. (2018, April 4) Facebook says data on most of Its 2 billion users Is vulnerable. *Bloomberg News*. Available online at www.bloomberg.com/news/articles/2018-04-04/facebook-says-data-on-87-million-people-may-have-been-shared.

Gabriel, E. (2018, July 27) Report: Kissinger urged Trump policy of pursuing Russia to contain China. *Mint Press News*. Available online at www.mintpress news.com/report-kissinger-urged-trump-policy-of-pursuing-russia-to-contain-china/246559.

Gallagher, R. and Greenwald, G. (2014, March 12) How the NSA plans to infect 'millions' of computers with malware. *The Intercept*. Available online at https://theintercept.com/2014/03/12/nsa-plans-infect-millions-computers-malware.

Garrie, A. (2018, March 22) Cambridge Analytica parent company hired by Ukrainian regime to spread fascism in Donbass: Russia must sanction company immediately. *Eurasiafuture.com*. Available online at www.eurasiafuture.com/2018/03/22/cambridge-analytica-parent-company-hired-by-ukrainian-regime-to-spread-fas cism-in-donbass-russia-must-sanction-company-immediately.

Giraldi, P. (2018, February 20) Russiagate suddenly becomes better. *The UNZ Review*. Available online at www.unz.com/pgiraldi/russiagate-suddenly-becomes-bigger.

Glaser, A. (2018, February 16) What we know about how Russia's IRA meddled in the 2016 Election. *Slate.com*. Available online at https://slate.com/technology/2018/02/what-we-know-about-the-internet-research-agency-and-how-it-med dled-in-the-2016-election.html.

Glikson, A. (2018, July 17) The mainstream media, the consequences of nuclear war and the drive toward WW III. *Global Research*. Available online at www.globalresearch.ca/the-mainstream-media-the-consequences-of-nuclear-war-and-the-drive-toward-ww-iii/5647729.

Global Economy (2018) Russia: Revenue minus production cost of oil, percent of GDP. *Globaleconomy.com*. Available online at www.theglobaleconomy.com/Russia/Oil_revenue/

Goldman, A. (2018, June 18) New charges in huge C.I.A. breach known as Vault 7. *The New York Times*. Available online at www.nytimes.com/2018/06/18/us/poli tics/charges-cia-breach-vault-7.html.

Goldman, A. and Haag, M. (2019, February 14) McCabe says Justice Dept. officials had discussions about pushing Trump out. *New York Times*. Available online at www.nytimes.com/2019/02/14/us/politics/mccabe-trump.html.

Gonzalez, A. and Lobo, A. (2018a, April 28) How Google, Facebook and Twitter are manipulating the Mexican presidential elections – Part 1. *World Socialist Web Site*. Available online at www.wsws.org/en/articles/2018/04/28/mex1-a28.html.

Gonzalez, A. and Lobo, A. (2018b, May 1) How Google, Facebook and Twitter are manipulating the Mexican presidential elections – Part 2. *World Socialist Web Site*. Available online at www.wsws.org/en/articles/2018/05/01/mexi-m01.html.

Goodman, J. (2018) The Man Who Knew Seth Rich – John Mark Dougan Speaks from Exile in Moscow. *Forbiddenknowledgetv.net*. Available online at https://for biddenknowledgetv.net/the-man-who-knew-seth-rich-john-mark-dougan-speaks-from-exile-in-moscow

Goldstein, L. (2018, September 25) A Critical Review of the Declassified Version of the Intelligence Community Assessment of Alleged "Russian Activities" in the

2016 US Elections. Available online at https://defyccc.com/wp-content/uploads/ICA_2017_01_commented_2018_09.pdf

Gordon, G., Condon, C. and S. Dunlap (2018, August 5) Georgia Election Officials Knew System Had 'Critical Vulnerabilities' Before 2016 Vote. *McClatchy D.C. Bureau*. Available online at www.mcclatchydc.com/news/politics-government/article216031450.html.

Gourarie, C. (2018, January 21) Censorship in the social media age. *Columbia Journalism Review*. Available online at www.cjr.org/analysis/censorship_in_the_social_media_age.php.

Gowans, S. (2017) *Washington's long war on Syria*. Montreal: Baraka Books.

Graff, G. (2018, February 20) Inside the Mueller indictment: A Russian novel of intrigue. *Wired.org*. Available online at www.wired.com/story/inside-the-mueller-indictment-a-russian-novel-of-intrigue.

Grassegger, H. and Krogerus, K. (2017, January 28) The data that turned the world upside down. *Vice.com*. Available online at https://motherboard.vice.com/en_us/article/mg9vvn/how-our-likes-helped-trump-win.

Greenwald, G. (2018, May 19) The FBI informant who monitored the Trump Campaign, Stefan Halper, oversaw a CIA spying operation in the 1980 presidential election. *The Intercept*. Available online at https://theintercept.com/2018/05/19/the-fbi-informant-who-monitored-the-trump-campaign-stefan-halper-oversaw-a-cia-spying-operation-in-the-1980-presidential-election/

Griffith, E. (2017, September 26) Facebook can absolutely control its algorithm. *Wired.com*. Available online at www.wired.com/story/facebook-can-absolutely-control-its-algorithm.

Gumbel, A. (2017, September 13) America's shameful history of voter suppression. *The Guardian*. Available online at www.theguardian.com/us-news/2017/sep/13/america-history-voter-suppression-donald-trump-election-fraud.

Haltiwanger, J. (2018, May 22) John McCain describes how he received the Steele dossier that contains the most salacious allegations about Trump and Russia. *Business Insider*. Available online at www.businessinsider.com/how-john-mccain-received-steele-dossier-trump-russia-2018-5.

Hannan, E. (2018, January 31) Garbage in, garbage out: Tech journalism, fake news and the Russia threat narrative. *Insurgeintelligence*. Available online at https://medium.com/insurge-intelligence/garbage-in-garbage-out-technology-journalism-as-a-microcosm-of-the-mass-media-crisis-93bd8a4ac37b.

Harding, L. (2017) *Collusion: Secret meetings, dirty money, and how Russia helped Donald Trump win*. New York: Vintage.

Harding, L. and Collyns, D. (2018, November 27) Manafort held secret talks with Assange in Ecuadorian embassy, sources say. *The Guardian*. Available online at www.theguardian.com/us-news/2018/nov/27/manafort-held-secret-talks-with-assange-in-ecuadorian-embassy.

Harris, S. (2017, June 29) GOP operative sought Clinton emails from hackers, implied a connection to Flynn. *Wall Street Journal*. Available online at www.wsj.com/articles/gop-operative-sought-clinton-emails-from-hackers-implied-a-connection-to-flynn-1498770851.

Hartmann, M. (2018, March 20) Facebook Haunted by Its Handling of 2016 Election Meddling. *New York Magazine*. Available online at http://nymag.com/daily/

intelligencer/2018/03/facebook-haunted-by-its-handling-of-2016-election-med dling.html

Hawkins, D. (2018, May 21) We surveyed 100 security experts. Almost all said state election systems were vulnerable. *Washington Post*. Available online at www. washingtonpost.com/news/powerpost/paloma/the-cybersecurity-202/2018/05/ 21/the-cybersecurity-202-we-surveyed-100-security-experts-almost-all-said-state-election-systems-were-vulnerable/5b0189b030fb0425887995e2/?noredirect= on&utm_term=.9404c7aa8efa.

Hayward, T. (2017, December 5) White Helmets: Who do they answer to? *Timhayward.wordpress.com*. Available online at https://timhayward.wordpress. com/2017/12/05/white-helmets-who-do-they-answer-to-2/

Heilbrunn, J. (2008) *They knew they were right. The rise of the neocons. An intellectual history of the neoconservative movement.* New York: Anchor.

Helmore, D. (2018, March 20) David Carroll, the US professor taking on Cambridge Analytica in the UK courts. *The Guardian*. Available online at www.theguardian.com/ uk-news/2018/mar/20/david-carroll-cambridge-analytica-uk-courts-us-professor.

Herb, J. (2018, July 4) Senate panel agrees with intel community that Putin was trying to help Trump. *CNN*. Available online at www.cnn.com/2018/07/03/politics/ senate-intelligence-putin-donald-trump/index.html.

Herman, E. and Peterson, D. (2007) The Dismantling of Yugoslavia (4 parts). *Monthly Review*. Available online at https://monthlyreview.org/2007/10/01/the-dismantling-of-yugoslavia.

Herman, Y. (2019, January 25) 'Largest scam in history': Half of Facebook accounts fake, says Zuckerberg's Harvard classmate. *Reuters*. Available online at www. rt.com/usa/449733-facebook-fake-users-report.

Hersh, S. (1968) *Chemical and biological warfare: America's hidden arsenal.* New York: Bobbs-Merrill; London: MacGibbon & Kee.

Hicks, C. (2016, November 7) Timeline of Hillary Clinton's email scandal. *CNN. com*. Available online at www.cnn.com/2016/10/28/politics/hillary-clinton-email-timeline/index.html.

Hilder, P. (2019, January 30) Explosive new tapes reveal Cambridge Analytica CEO's boasts of voter suppression, manipulation and bribery. *Open Democracy*. Available online at www.opendemocracy.net/brexitinc/paul-hilder/they-were-planning-on-stealing-election-explosive-new-tapes-reveal-cambridg.

Hindman, M. (2018, March 30) How Cambridge Analytica's Facebook targeting model really worked – according to the person who built it. *The Conversation*. Available online at http://theconversation.com/how-cambridge-analyticas-facebook-targeting-model-really-worked-according-to-the-person-who-built-it-94078.

Holm, E. (2014) Social networking and identity theft in the digital society. *The International Journal on Advances in Life Sciences*, 6 (3&4):157–166, ISSN 1942-2660.

Hornberger, J. (2018a, December 17) Butina pleads guilty to befriending the US. *Information Clearing House*. Available online at www.informationclearinghouse. info/50779.htm.

Hornberger, J. (2018b, July 17) Mueller's indictment Isn't worth squat. *The Future of Freedom Foundation*. Available online at www.fff.org/2018/07/16/ muellers-indictment-isnt-worth-squat.

Horvitz, J. (2018, June 15) Trump 2020 working with ex-Cambridge Analytica staffers. *CNBC.com*. Available online at www.cnbc.com/2018/06/15/trump-2020-working-with-ex-cambridge-analytica-staffers.html.

House of Commons (2018, July 29) "*Disinformation and 'fake news': Interim Report*". House of Commons. Digital, Culture, Media and Sport Committee. Available online at https://publications.parliament.uk/pa/cm201719/cmselect/cmcumeds/363/363.pdf

House Permanent Select Committee on Intelligence (HPSCI) (2018) *Report on active Russian measures*. U.S. House of Representatives, Washington D.C.

Howard, P.N., Ganesh, B., Liotsiou, D., Kelly, J. & and François, C. (2018) *The IRA, social media and political polarization in the USA (2012–2018)*. Computational Propaganda Research Project. London and New York: Oxford University Press.

Howard, P.N. and Woolley, S. (2016) Political communication, computational propaganda, and autonomous agents. *International Journal of Communication*, 10 (Special Issue), 4882–4890.

Ike, S. (2018, May 4) Facebook has already removed millions of pieces of terrorist content in 2018. *Aplus.com*. Available online at https://aplus.com/a/facebook-terrorist-content-artificial-intelligence.

Illing, S. (2018, April 4) Cambridge Analytica, the shady data firm that might be a key Trump-Russia link, explained. *Vox*. Available online at www.vox.com/policy-and-politics/2017/10/16/15657512/cambridge-analytica-facebook-alexander-nix-christopher-wylie.

Investor's Business Daily (2018) Funny, when Obama harvested Facebook data on millions of users to win in 2012, everyone cheered. *Investor's Business Daily*. Available online at www.investors.com/politics/editorials/facebook-data-scandal-trump-election-obama-2012.

Isaac, M. (2018, January 11) Facebook overhauls news feed to focus on what friends and family share. *The New York Times*. Available online at www.nytimes.com/2018/01/11/technology/facebook-news-feed.html.

James, S. (2018, July 20) UK poisonings: New allegations expose more contradictions. *Global Research*. Available online at www.globalresearch.ca/uk-poisonings-new-allegations-expose-more-contradictions/5648215.

Jamieson, K.H. (2018) *Cyberwar. How Russian hackers and trolls helped elect a president what we don't, can't, and do know*. London and New York: Oxford University Press.

Janjevic, D. (2018, April 6) The curious case of Yulia Skripal's recorded phone call. *Deutsche Welle*. Available online at www.dw.com/en/the-curious-case-of-yulia-skripals-recorded-phone-call/a-43287554.

Jankowski, N. (2018) Researching fake news: A selective examination of empirical studies. *Javnost – The Public*, 25:1–2, 248–255, DOI: 10.1080/13183222.2018.1418964.

Johnstone, C. (2018a, March 4) Social media censorship Is vastly more dangerous than the censored material. *Medium*. Available online at https://medium.com/@caityjohnstone/social-media-censorship-is-vastly-more-dangerous-than-the-censored-material-a9d467ccf738

Johnstone, C. (2018b, April 8) New Syrian chemical weapons attack being reported by all the usual suspects. *Medium*. Available online at https://medium.com/

@caityjohnstone/new-syrian-chemical-weapons-attack-being-reported-by-all-the-usual-suspects-bb52e9a4f982

Johnstone, C. (2018c, October 11) Anti-Media shut down by Facebook and Twitter. *The Investigative*. Available online at https://theinvestigative.ooo/anti-media-shut-down-by-facebook-and-twitter

Johnstone, C. (2018d, December 17) Mass media's Russia hysteria is openly acknowledging the power of propaganda. *Mike Norman Economics*. Available online at http://mikenormaneconomics.blogspot.com/2018/12/caitlin-johnstone-mass-medias-russia.html

Johnson, J. (2018e, May 21) Media ignore government influence on Facebook's plan to fight government influence. FAIR.org. Available online at https://fair.org/home/media-ignore-government-influence-on-facebooks-plan-to-fight-government-influence.

Joseph, S. (2018, April 2) Why the business model of social media giants like Facebook is incompatible with human rights. *The Conversation*. Available online at https://theconversation.com/why-the-business-model-of-social-media-giants-like-facebook-is-incompatible-with-human-rights-94016

Jowett, G. and O'Donnell (2014) *Propaganda and persuasion*. 6th edition. Thousand Oaks, CA: Sage.

Judicial Watch (2018) FBI records show Russian dossier author deemed 'not suitable for use' as source, show several FBI payments in 2016. *Judicialwatch.org*. Available online at www.judicialwatch.org/press-room/press-releases/judicial-watch-fbi-records-show-dossier-author-deemed-not-suitable-for-use-as-source-show-several-fbi-payments-in-2016.

Kazeem, Y. (2018, March 22) Cambridge Analytica tried to sway Nigeria's last elections with Buhari's hacked emails. *Quartz*. Available online at https://qz.com/1234916/cambridge-analytica-tried-to-sway-nigerias-last-elections-with-buharis-hacked-emails.

Keefer, M. (2017, January 15) Our Man in London: The Scandal of the 35-Page 'Intelligence Dossier' Directed against Donald Trump. *GlobalResearch.ca* Available online at www.globalresearch.ca/our-man-in-london-the-scandal-of-the-35-page-intelligence-dossier-directed-against-donald-trump/5568555.

Keller, M. (2018, August 11) The flourishing business of fake YouTube views. *New York Times*. Available online at www.nytimes.com/interactive/2018/08/11/technology/youtube-fake-view-sellers.html.

Kessler, G. (2018, January 9) What you need to know about Christopher Steele, the FBI and the Trump 'dossier. *Washington Post*. Available online at www.washingtonpost.com/news/fact-checker/wp/2018/01/09/what-you-need-to-know-about-christopher-steele-the-fbi-and-the-dossier/?utm_term=.129fe15c462e.

Keys, D. (2015, July 9) How the British Government subjected thousands of people to chemical and biological warfare trials during Cold War. *The Independent*. Available online at www.independent.co.uk/news/uk/politics/how-the-british-government-subjected-thousands-of-people-to-chemical-and-biological-warfare-trials-10376411.html.

Kharpal, A. (2018, March 25) Facebook rolls out its first changes since Mark Zuckerberg promised to 'do better.' *CNBC*. Available online at www.cnbc.com/2018/03/28/facebook-unveils-new-privacy-tools-to-let-you-control-your-data-better.html.

Kiriakou, J. (2018, August 4) After Snowden. *Reader Support News*. Available online at https://readersupportednews.org/opinion2/277-75/51551-rsn-after-snowden.

Kirkpatrick, D. (2018, June 14) Who is behind Trump's links to Arab princes? A billionaire friend. *The New York Times*. Available online at www.nytimes.com/2018/06/13/world/middleeast/trump-tom-barrack-saudi.html

Klare, M. (2018a, June 19) Is a war with China on the horizon? *Truthdig*. Available online at www.truthdig.com/articles/is-a-war-with-china-on-the-horizon.

Klare, M. (2018b, July 24) Trump's grand strategy. *The Nation*. Available online at www.tomdispatch.com/post/176451/tomgram:_michael_klare,_trump%27s_grand_strategy.

Klarenberg, K. (2019, February 7) How integrity initiative's 'counterfeit expert' perpetuated novichok narrative. *Sputnik News*. Available online at https://sputniknews.com/world/201902071072221113-kaszeta-integrity-initiative-novichok/

Klein, E. (2017, November 14) Was the democratic primary rigged? *Vox*. Available online at www.vox.com/policy-and-politics/2017/11/14/16640082/donna-brazile-warren-bernie-sanders-democratic-primary-rigged.

Knip, K., (2018, March 21) 'Unknown' newcomer Novichok was long known. *NRC.NL*. Available online at www.nrc.nl/nieuws/2018/03/21/unknown-newcomer-Novichok-was-long-known-a1596490.

Konkel, F. (2014, July 17) The details about the CIA's deal with Amazon. *The Atlantic*. Available online at www.theatlantic.com/technology/archive/2014/07/the-details-about-the-cias-deal-with-amazon/374632.

Kottasová, I. (2018, May 2) Russian military spending drops for first time in 20 years. *CNN*. Available online at http://money.cnn.com/2018/05/02/news/russia-defense-spending-plunge/index.html.

Kristensen, H. McKinzie, M. and T. Postol (2017, March 1) How US nuclear force modernization is undermining strategic stability: The burst-height compensating super-fuze. *Bulletin of the Atomic Scientists*. Available online at https://thebulletin.org/how-us-nuclear-force-modernization-undermining-strategic-stability-burst-height-compensating-super10578.

Laforgia, M. and Dance, G. (2018, June 5) Facebook gave data access to Chinese firm flagged by U.S. intelligence. *The New York Times*. Available online at www.nytimes.com/2018/06/05/.../facebook-device-partnerships-china.html.

Lapowsky, I. (2017, October 26) What did Cambridge Analytica really do for Trump's campaign? *Wired.org*. Available online at www.wired.com/story/what-did-cambridge-analytica-really-do-for-trumps-campaign/

Latin Library (nd) The Yalta conference (1945) *thelatinlibary.com*. Available online at www.thelatinlibrary.com/imperialism/notes/yalta.html.

Lawrence, P. (2017, August 9) A new report raises big questions about last year's DNC hack. *The Nation*. Available online at www.thenation.com/article/a-new-report-raises-big-questions-about-last-years-dnc-hack.

Lee, M., Timbereg, C. and J. Dawsey. (2018, March 23) Cambridge Analytica harnessed Facebook data in work for super PAC led by John Bolton, according to former employees. *The Washington Post*. Available online at www.washingtonpost.com/

Leetaru, K. (2016, December 22) The Daily Mail Snopes story and fact checking the fact checkers. *Forbes.com*. Available online at www.forbes.com/sites/kalevleetaru/2016/12/22/the-daily-mail-snopes-story-and-fact-checking-the-fact-checkers/#2ecb5b83227f.

Leonnig, C., Entous, A., Barrett, D. and M. Zapotosky (2017, December 1) Michael Flynn pleads guilty to lying to FBI on contacts with Russian ambassador. *Washington Post*. Available online at www.washingtonpost.com/politics/michael-flynn-charged-with-making-false-statement-to-the-fbi/2017/12/01/e03a6c48-d6a2-11e7-9461-ba77d604373d_story.html?utm_term=.2c72a8b5e4fa.

Levintova, H. (2017, October 18) Russian journalists just published a bombshell investigation about a Kremlin-linked "Troll Factory." *Mother Jones*. Available online at www.motherjones.com/politics/2017/10/russian-journalists-just-published-a-bombshell-investigation-about-a-kremlin-linked-troll-factory.

Levintova, H. (2018, November 29) If accused Russian spy Maria Butina sings, here's what she might tell the Feds. *Mother Jones*. Available at www.motherjones.com/politics/2018/11/marina-butina-plea-agreement-coming.

Lewis, P (2018, March 23) Trump adviser John Bolton worked with Cambridge Analytica on YouTube voter experiment. *The Guardian*. Available online at www.theguardian.com/us-news/2018/mar/23/john-bolton-cambridge-analytica-videos-donald-trump.

Link, G. (2018, June 18) NATO, Germany build up for war against Russia. *World Socialist Web Site*. Available online at www.wsws.org/en/articles/2018/06/18/bund-j18.htm.

London, E. (2018 July 20) What is "our democracy"? *World Socialist Web Site*. Available online at www.google.com/search?q=London%2C+E.+%282018+July+20%29+What+is+%E2%80%9Cour+democracy%E2%80%9D%3F+World+Socialist+Web+Site&ie=utf-8&oe=utf-8&client=firefox-b-1.

Lynch, S. (2018, September 10) U.S. judge orders accused Russian agent Butina kept in jail. *Reuters*. Available online at www.reuters.com/article/us-usa-russia-butina/u-s-judge-orders-accused-russian-agent-butina-kept-in-jail-idUSKCN1LQ1VS.

Macaray, D. (2018, May 1) Where it all began. The dawn of "Fake News." *Counterpunch.org*. Available online at www.counterpunch.org/2018/05/01/where-it-all-began-the-dawn-of-fake-news.

MacAskill, E. (2017, May 5) The CIA has a long history of helping to kill leaders around the world. *The Guardian*. Available online at www.theguardian.com/us-news/2017/may/05/cia-long-history-kill-leaders-around-the-world-north-korea.

MacAskill, E. and Dance, G. (2013, November 1) NSA files decoded: What the revelations mean for you. *The Guardian*. Available online at www.theguardian.com/world/interactive/2013/nov/01/snowden-nsa-files-surveillance-revelations-decoded#section/1.

Macilwain, D. (2018, October 15) The framing of Russia. *Information Clearing House*. Available online at www.informationclearinghouse.info/50448.htm.

Mackey, R. (2017, November 15) Julian Assange's hatred of Hillary Clinton was no secret. His advice to Donald Trump was. *The Intercept*. Available online at https://theintercept.com/2017/11/15/wikileaks-julian-assange-donald-trump-jr-hillary-clinton.

Mackie, T. (2017, October 28) US forces destroy deadly ISIS chemical weapons uncovered in Iraq and Syria as jihadis flee. *Express*. Available online at www.express.co.uk/news/world/872209/isis-jihadis-terrorism-raqqa-syria-iraq-us-chemical-weapons-war.

Mackinder, H. (2004) The geopolitical pivot of history. *The Geographical Journal*, Vol. 23, No.4, (April 1904), 421–437.

Madrigal, A. (2018, February 19) Russia's troll operation was not that sophisticated. *The Atlantic*. Available online at www.theatlantic.com/technology/archive/2018/02/the-russian-conspiracy-to-commit-audience-development/553685/

Maheshwari, S. (2018, March 12) Uncovering Instagram bots with a new kind of detective work. *New York Times*. Available online at www.nytimes.com/2018/03/12/business/media/instagram-bots.html.

Malm, S. (2018) Oligarch Boris Berezovsky was killed by British intelligence to stop him returning to Russia and revealing information he'd learned while working with UK spies, says Moscow's top prosecutor. *Daily Mail*. Available online at www.dailymail.co.uk/news/article-5629315/Boris-Berezovsky-killed-decided-return-Russia-Moscow-prosecutor.html.

Marketwatch (2018, February 20) Trump seizes on tweets by Facebook executive as proof Russia didn't tilt election to him. *Marketwatch*. Available online at www.marketwatch.com/story/trump-seizes-on-tweets-by-facebook-executive-as-proof-russia-didnt-tilt-election-to-him-2018, February 17.

Martyanov, A. (2018) *Losing military supremacy: The myopia of American strategic planning*. Atlanta, GA: Clarity Press.

Maté, A. (2018a, June 13) The Mueller indictments still don't add up to collusion. *The Nation*. Available online at www.thenation.com/article/mueller-indictments-still-dont-add-collusion.

Maté, A. (2018b, December 17) New studies show pundits are wrong about Rissan social-media involvement in US politics. *The Nation*. Available online at www.thenation.com/article/russiagate-elections-interference.

Maté, A. (2019, January 11) The Manafort revelation is not a smoking gun. *The Nation*. Available online at www.thenation.com/article/manafort-no-smoking-gun-collusion.

Matlock, J. (2018, July 3) Former US envoy to Moscow calls intelligence report on alleged Russian interference 'politically motivated'. *Consortiumnews.com*. Available online at https://consortiumnews.com/2018/07/03/former-us-envoy-to-moscow-calls-intelligence-report-on-alleged-russian-interference-politically-motivated.

Mayer, J. (2018, March 12) Christopher Steele, the man behind the Trump dossier. *The New Yorker*. Available online at www.newyorker.com/magazine/2018/03/12/christopher-steele-the-man-behind-the-trump-dossier.

McCarthy, A. (2019, January 29) Stone indictment underscores that there was no Trump-Russia conspiracy. *National Review*. Available online at www.nationalreview.com/2019/01/roger-stone-indictment-underscores-no-trump-russia-conspiracy/

McCarthy, T. (2017, December 8) CNN forced to climb down over Trump-Wiki-Leaks email report. *The Guardian*. Available online at www.theguardian.com/us-news/2017/dec/08/trump-email-key-wikileaks-hacked-documents.

McCoy, A. (2009) *Policing America's empire: The United States, the Philippines, and the rise of the surveillance state*. Madison: University of Wisconsin Press.

McCoy, A. (2017) *In the shadows of the American century. The rise and decline of US global power*. Chicago: Haymarket.

McCoy, A. (2018) Is a modern Chinese navy a threat to the United States? *The Nation*. Available online at www.thenation.com/article/is-a-modern-chinese-navy-a-threat-to-the-united-states/

McFaul, M. (2005) *American efforts at promoting regime change in the Soviet Union and then Russia: Lessons learned*. Stanford, CA: Centre on Democracy, Development and Rule of Law (CDDRL) Working Papers, Stanford Institute on International Studies.

McGovern, R. (2018a, June 7) Still waiting for evidence of a Russian hack. *Consortiumnews.com*. Available online at https://consortiumnews.com/2018/06/07/still-waiting-for-evidence-of-a-russian-hack.

McGovern, R. (2018b, June 27) Did Sen. Warner and Comey 'Collude' on Russia-gate? *Consortiumnews.com*. Available online at https://consortiumnews.com/2018/06/27/did-sen-warner-and-comey-collude-on-russia-gate.

McGovern, R. (2018c, July 23) Moon-Strzok no more, Lisa Page spills the beans. *Consortiumnews.com*. Available online at https://consortiumnews.com/2018/07/23/moon-strzok-no-more-lisa-page-spills-the-beans/

McGovern, R. (2018d, December 20) Michael Isikoff cuts his losses at Russian routlette. *Consortium News*. Available online at https://consortiumnews.com/2018/12/19/michael-isikoff-cuts-his-loses-at-russian-roulette.

McKeigue, P. (2018, July 2) Notes on alleged use in Syria of chlorine and sarin together. Private communication.

McKeigue, P., Larson, A. and Mason, J. (2018 August) Briefing note: The alleged chemical attack in Douma on 7 April 2018, and other alleged chlorine attacks in *Syria. Working Group on Syria Propaganda and Media*. Available online at http://syriapropagandamedia.org.

McKeigue, P., Miller, D. and P.Robinson (2019) The Organisation for the Prohibition of Chemical Weapons (OPCW): critical questions. Working Group on Syria Propaganda and Media. Available online at https://timhayward.wordpress.com/2019/04/12/the-organisation-for-the-prohibition-of-chemical-weapons-opcw-critical-questions/.

McKeigue, P., Miller, D., Mason, J. and P. Robinson. (2018, December) The integrity initiative. *Working Group on Syria, Propaganda and Media*. Available online at http://syriapropagandamedia.org/the-integrity-initiative.

McKeigue, P., and P. Robinson (2018) Doubts about "Novichoks" Working Group on Syria, Propaganda and Media. Available online at http://syriapropaganda media.org/working-papers.

Mearsheimer, J. and Walt, S (2008) *The Israel Lobby and US Foreign Policy*. New York: Farrar, Straus and Giroux.

Mearsheimer, J. and Walt, S. (2017) *The Israel lobby and U.S. foreign policy*. New York: Farrar, Straus and Giroux.

MediaLens (2018 July 17) No nerve agents found – The OPCW Interim Report on Douma. *Medialens.org*. Available online at http://medialens.org/index.php/alerts/alert-archive/2018/874-no-nerve-agents-found-the-opcw-interim-report-on-douma.html.

Mendick, R, Dixon, H, Sawer, P and L. Heighton (2018, March 7) Poisoned Russian spy Sergei Skripal was close to consultant who was linked to the Trump dossier. *The Telegraph.* Available online at www.telegraph.co.uk/news/2018/03/07/poisoned-russian-spy-sergei-skripal-close-consultant-linked.

Mercouris, A. (2014, December 3) The importance of the cancellation of South Stream. *The Saker.* Available online at http://thesaker.is/the-importance-of-the-cancellation-of-south-stream/comment-page-3.

Mercouris, A. (2017, December 12) The Litvinenko inquiry – a legal critique and alternative view. *Off Guardian.* Available online at https://off-guardian.org/2017/12/12/the-litvinenko-inquiry-a-legal-critique-and-alternative-view.

Meyer, J. (2018, November 17) New evidence emerges of Steve Banon and Cambridge Analytica's rokle in Brexit. *The New Yorker* Available online at www.newyorker.com/news/news-desk/new-evidence-emerges-of-steve-bannon-and-cambridge-analyticas-role-in-brexit.

Miller, J. (1999, May 25) US and Uzbeks agree on chemical arms plant cleanup. *New York Times.* Available online at www.nytimes.com/1999/05/25/world/us-and-uzbeks-agree-on-chemical-arms-plant-cleanup.html.

Mirzayanov, V. S. (2008) *State Secrets: An Insider's Chronicle of the Russian Chemical Weapons Program.* Denver, CO: Outskirts Press.

Moon of Alabama (2018a, February 17) Mueller Indictment – The "Russian Influence" Is A Commercial Marketing Scheme. *Moon of Alabama.* Available online at www.moonofalabama.org/2018/02/mueller-indictement-the-russian-influence-is-a-commercial-marketing-scheme.html.

Moon of Alabama (2018b, December 18) Senate reports on "Russian Information Campaign" fail to discuss its only known motive. *MoonofAlabama.* Available online at www.moonofalabama.org/2018/12/senate-reports-on-russian-influence-campaign-fail-to-discuss-its-only-known-motive.html.

Moran, J. (2013) Conspiracy and contemporary history: Revisiting MI5 and the Wilson plot[s]. *Journal of Intelligence History*, 13:2, 161–175, DOI: 10.1080/16161262.2014.896112.

Morris, D. (2018, February 17) How Russians used social media to boost the Trump campaign, according to Robert Mueller's indictment. *Fortune.com.* Available online at http://fortune.com/2018/02/17/how-russians-used-social-media-election.

Morris, S. and Crerar, P. (2018, April 3) Porton Down experts unable to verify precise source of Novichok. *The Guardian* Available online at www.theguardian.com/uk-news/2018/apr/03/porton-down-experts-unable-to-verify-precise-source-of-Novichok.

Morrow, W. (2018a, May 30) Amazon, Microsoft and Google compete for Pentagon Cloud warfighter project. *World Socialist Web Site.* Available online at www.wsws.org/en/articles/2018/05/30/jedi-m30.html.

Morrow, W. (2018b, December 31) US intelligence think tank conducted false flag operation impersonating Russian election interference. *World Socialist Web Site.* Available online at www.wsws.org/en/articles/2018/12/31/know-d31.html.

Morse, J. (2018, March 20) Cambridge Analytica had a tech-savvy strategy to destroy potential evidence. *Mashable.* Available online at https://mashable.com/2018/03/20/cambridge-analytica-protonmail-erasing-email/#rWGGLabaVqqB.

Murdock, J. (2018, May 3) What is Emerdata? As Cambridge Analytica shuts, directors surface in new firm. *Newsweek.* Available online at www.newsweek.

com/what-emerdata-scl-group-executives-flee-new-firm-and-its-registered-office-909334.

Murray, C. (2017, July 3) The stink without a secret. *Craigmurray.com*. Available online at www.craigmurray.org.uk/archives/2017/07/stink-without-secret.

Murray, C. (2018a, March 17) First recorded successful Novichok synthesis was in 2016 – by Iran, in cooperation with the OPCW. *Global Research*. Available online at www.globalresearch.ca/first-recorded-successful-Novichok-synthesis-was-in-2016-by-iran-in-cooperation-with-the-opcw/5632581.

Murray, C. (2018b, April 30) Where they tell you not to look. *Craigmurray.org*. Available online at www.craigmurray.org.uk/archives/2018/04/where-they-tell-you-not-to-look/comment-page-4/

National Security Archive (2017, December 17) NATO expansion: What Gorbachev heard. *Nsarchive.gwu.com*. Available online at https://nsarchive.gwu.edu/briefing-book/russia-programs/2017-12-12/nato-expansion-what-gorbachev-heard-west ern-leaders-early.

Nebehay, S. (2018, June 20) Both sides committed war crimes during siege of Syria's Ghouta: U.N. *Reuters*. Available online at www.reuters.com/article/us-mideast-crisis-syria-warcrimes/both-sides-committed-war-crimes-during-siege-of-syrias-ghouta-un-idUSKBN1JG15I

News Front (2018 September) Skripal case: Israeli expert on the work of the special agents. *News Front*. Available online at https://en.news-front.info/2018/09/28/skripal-case-israeli-expert-on-the-work-of-the-special-agents.

Nord, R. (2018a July 3) Cambridge Analytica's parent company used Yemen as psyop test site, *Blacklistednews.com*. Available online at www.blacklistednews.com/article/66877/cambridge-analyticas-parent-company-used-yemen-as-psyop-test.html.

Nord, R. (2018b) Saudis move to behead female activist as Facebook censors anti-Saudi content. *MintPressNews.com*. Available online at www.mintpressnews.com/saudi-arabia-behead-activist/248162.

Nyhan, B. (2018, February 13) Fake news and bots may be worrisome, but their political power Is overblown. *New York Times*. Available online at www.nytimes.com/2018/02/13/upshot/fake-news-and-bots-may-be-worrisome-but-their-politi cal-power-is-overblown.html.

O'Brien, L. and Stein, A. (2018, June 15) The military logic behind Assad's use of chemical weapons. *Warontherocks.com*. Available online at https://warontherocks.com/2018/06/the-military-logic-behind-assads-use-of-chemical-weapons.

O'Hare, L. (2018, March 20) SCL – A very British coup. *Bella Caledonia*. Available online at https://bellacaledonia.org.uk/2018/03/20/scl-a-very-british-coup.

O'Neill, J. (2018a, March 13) The strange case of the Russian spy poisoning. *Consortiumnews.com*. Available online at https://consortiumnews.com/2018/03/13/the-strange-case-of-the-russian-spy-poisoning.

O'Neill, J. (2018b, September 26) MH17: Some truth emerging at last. *New Eastern Outlook*. Available online at https://journal-neo.org/2018/09/26/mh17-some-truth-emerging-at-last.

O'Sullivan, D. and Griffin, D. (2018a, March 23) Ex-Cambridge Analytica staff say Bolton super PAC used compromised Facebook data. *CNN.com*. Available online at www.cnn.com/2018/03/23/politics/john-bolton-super-pac-cambridge-analytica/index.html.

O'Sullivan, D. and Griffin, D. (2018b, May 17) Cambridge Analytica ran voter suppression campaigns, whistleblower claims. *CNN.com*. Available online at www.cnn.com/2018/05/16/politics/cambridge-analytica-congress-wylie/index.html.

Office of the Director of National Intelligence (ODNI) (2017) *Assessing Russian activities and intentions in recent US elections*. ODNI. Available online at www.dni.gov/files/documents/ICA_2017_01.pd.

Office of the Inspector General (2018, June) *A review of various actions by the Federal Bureau of Investigation and Department of Justice in advance of the 2016 election*. U.S. Department of Justice. Oversight and Review Division. Washington D.C.

Organization for the Prohibition of Chemical Weapons (OPCW) (2018, July 6) *OPCW Issues Fact-Finding Mission Reports on Chemical Weapons Use Allegations in Douma, Syria in 2018 and in Al-Hamadaniya and Karm Al-Tarrab in 2016*. OPCW.org. Available online from www.opcw.org/news/article/opcw-issues-fact-finding-mission-reports-on-chemical-weapons-use-allegations-in-douma-syria-in-2018-and-in-al-hamadaniya-and-karm-al-tarrab-in-2016/

Organization for the Prohibition of Chemical Weapons (OPCW) (2016, January 4) *Destruction of declared Syrian chemical weapons completed*. Opcw.org. Available online at www.opcw.org/news/article/destruction-of-syrian-chemical-weapons-completed.

Organization for the Prohibition of Chemical Weapons (OPCW) (2017, October 11) *OPCW Marks Completion of Destruction of Russian Chemical Weapons Stockpile*. Opcw.org. Available online at www.opcw.org/news/article/opcw-marks-completion-of-destruction-of-russian-chemical-weapons-stockpile.

Ortutay, B. (2018, March 25) What Facebook's privacy policy allows may surprise you. *APNews.com*. Available online at https://apnews.com/8e78b38f0b1744299b6d144e6c738002.

Palast, G. (2017, November 1) Crosscheck overwhelmingly purges legitimate voters, new study finds researchers From Stanford, Harvard, Yale, Penn, and Microsoft independently corroborate our work. *GregPalast.com*. Available online at www.gregpalast.com/crosscheck-overwhelmingly-purges-legitimate-voters.

Palast, G. (2018, March 19) Cambridge Analytica ain't nuthin:Look out For i360 and DataTrust. *GregPalast.com*. Available online at www.gregpalast.com/cambridge-analytica-aint-nuthin-look-i360-datatrust/

Parry, R. (2017, June 8) A pack of excuses and the '17 intelligence agencies' falsehood. Consortiumnews.com. republished in *TruthDig.com*. Available online at www.truthdig.com/articles/a-pack-of-excuses-and-the-17-intelligence-agencies-falsehood.

Patterson, D. (2018, November 26) Why voting machines in the U.S. are easy targets for hackers. *CBS News*. Available online at www.cbsnews.com/news/why-voting-machines-in-the-u-s-are-easy-targets-for-hackers.

Peries, S. (2018, August 3) Oxford study: Political data mining companies are manipulating elections around the world. *Real News Network*. Available online at https://therealnews.com/stories/oxford-study-political-data-mining-companies-are-manipulating-elections-around-the-world.

Pilger, J. (2014, October 23) The British-American coup that ended Australian independence. *The Guardian*. Available online at www.theguardian.com/commentisfree/2014/oct/23/gough-whitlam-1975-coup-ended-australian-independence.

Pinchuk, D. and Busvine, D. (2018, March 21) Academic in Facebook storm worked on Russian 'dark' personality project. *Reuters.com*. Available online at www. reuters.com/article/uk-facebook-cambridge-analytica-kogan/academic-in-facebook-storm-worked-on-russian-dark-personality-project-idUKKBN1 GX2F8.

Pitt, B. (2018, June 27) Seymour Hersh and massacres – the degeneration of a respected journalist. *Medium*. Available online at https://medium.com/@pitt_bob/seymour-hersh-and-massacres-the-degeneration-of-a-respected-journalist-dda5929c1b67.

Porter, G. (2018, October 10) The shaky case that Russia manipulated social media to tip the 2016 Election. *Consortium News*. Available online at https://consortiumnews.com/2018/10/10/the-shaky-case-that-russia-manipulated-social-media-to-tip-the-2016-election/.

Press Association (2019, January 20) Novichok poisoning victims first helped by teenage girl. *The Guardian*. Available online at www.theguardian.com/uk-news/2019/jan/20/novichok-poisoning-victims-sergei-skripal-first-helped-by-teenage-girl.

Preza, E. (2018, June 17) Trump confidant Roger Stone admits he met with a Russian offering dirt on Hillary Clinton during the 2016 campaign. *Washington Post*. Available online at www.washingtonpost.com/.../trump-associate-roger-stone...russian-national-durin

Price, G. (2018, March 8) Poisoned Russian spy linked to Trump-Russia Dossier author Christopher Steele through security consultant. *Newsweek.com*. Available online at www.newsweek.com/russia-poison-spy-steele-dossier-836768.

Price, R. and Sheth, S. (2018, March 22) DNC hacker 'Guccifer 2.0' was reportedly confirmed as a Russian agent after forgetting to conceal his identity online. *Business Insider*. Available online at www.businessinsider.com/dnc-hacker-guccifer-confirmed-as-russian-agent-after-forgetting-to-conceal-identity-2018–3.

Privy Counsellors (2016) *The report of the Iraq inquiry* (The Chilcott Report). Westminster, London: House of Commons.

Prokop, A. (2017, August 25) Robert Mueller is looking into Michael Flynn's potential ties to Russian hackers. *Vox*. Available online at www.vox.com/2017/6/29/15896582/trump-russia-michael-flynn-wsj.

Prokop, A. (2018a, May 2) Cambridge Analytica shutting down: The firm's many scandals, explained. *Vox*. Available online at www.vox.com/policy-and-politics/2018/3/21/17141428/cambridge-analytica-trump-russia-mueller.

Prokop, A. (2018b July 18) Maria Butina, explained: The accused Russian spy who tried to sway US politics through the NRA. *Vox.com*. Available online at www.vox.com/2018/7/19/17581354/maria-butina-russia-nra-trump.

Quinton, S. (2018, December 7) Lame-duck power grabs escalate unsettling trend. *Pew Trusts*. Available online at www.pewtrusts.org/en/research-and-analysis/blogs/stateline/2018/12/07/lame-duck-power-grabs-escalate-unsettling-trend.

Re, G. (2018, December 20) McCain associate shared unverified Steele dossier with Buzzfeed, court filing says. *Fox News*. Available online at www.foxnews.com/politics/mccain-associate-gave-unverified-steele-dossier-to-buzzfeed-court-filing-says.

Read, M (2018, December 26) How m,uch of the Internet is fake? Turns out, a lot of it, actually. *The Intelligencer*. Available online at http://nymag.com/intel ligencer/2018/12/how-much-of-the-internet-is-fake.html.

Real News Network (2018, February 22) Russian espionage of clickbait? *Real News Network*. Available online at https://therealnews.com/stories/russian-espionage-or-clickbait-1-2.

Reed, K. (2018, November 8) Facebook and Twitter intensify censorship in 2018 elections. *World Socialist Web Site*. Available online at www.wsws.org/en/arti cles/2018/11/08/face-n08.html.

Richman, S. (2018, July 24) Trump and Putin: How about getting rid of your nuke? *Counterpunch.org*. Available online at www.counterpunch.org/2018/07/24/ trump-and-putin-how-about-getting-rid-of-your-nukes.

Riddle, T. (2017, March 22) Red Don, Russian mobsters and Putin's playground. *Deep Politics Forum*. Available online at https://deeppoliticsforum.com/forums/ showthread.php?16414-Red-Don-Russian-mobsters-and-Putin-s-Playground#. Wym5biAnaCo.

Ritter, S. (2016, December 12) The 'slam dunk' that isn't – The CIA, Russia and the hacking Of The 2016 presidential election. *Huffington Post*. Available online at www.huffingtonpost.com/entry/cia-russia-dnc-hacking_us_584f535ee4b0bd9 c3dfe722e.

Ritter, S. (2017, July 28) Time to Reassess the Roles Played by Guccifer 2.0 and Russia in the DNC 'Hack. *Truthdig.org*. Available online at www.truthdig.com/ articles/time-to-reassess-the-roles-played-by-guccifer-2-0-and-russia-in-the-dnc-hack/

Ritter, S. (2018a, January 8) In the Russian collusion debate, Who's fooling who? *The American Conservative*. Available online at www.theamericanconservative. com/articles/in-the-russian-collusion-debate-whos-fooling-who/

Ritter, S. (2018b, March 22) No, Putin isn't bluffing on nukes. *The American Conservative*. Available online at www.theamericanconservative.com/articles/no-put in-isnt-bluffing-on-nukes/

Ritter, S. (2018c, July 17) Indictment of 12 Russians: Under the shiny wrapping, a political act. *Truthdig.com*. Available online at www.truthdig.com/articles/ indictment-of-12-russians-under-the-shiny-wrapping-a-political-act.

Roose, K. (2018, March 19) How Facebook's data sharing went from feature to bug. *The New York Times*. Available online at www.nytimes.com/2018/03/19/technol ogy/facebook-data-sharing.html.

Root, E. (1916/2019) *Addresses on international subjects*. UK: Wentworth Press.

Rosenberg, M. (2018, March 23) Bolton was early beneficiary of Cambridge Analytica's Facebook data. *New York Times*. Available online at www.nytimes. com/2018/03/23/us/politics/bolton-cambridge-analyticas-facebook-data.html.

Rosenberg, M., Confessore, N. and Cadwalladr, C. (2018, April 4) Cambridge Analytica and Facebook: The scandal and the fallout so far. *New York Times*. Available online at www.nytimes.com/2018/04/04/us/politics/cambridge-analy tica-scandal-fallout.html.

Ross, C. (2018, May 17) Cambridge Prof with CIA, MI6 ties met with Trump adviser during campaign, beyond. *The Daily Caller*. Available online at https:// dailycaller.com/2018/05/17/halper-trump-page-papadopoulos/

Rotella, S. (2018, January 19) Russian Politician Who Reportedly Sent Millions to NRA Has Long History in Spain. *ProPublica*. Available online at www.pro publica.org/article/russian-politician-who-reportedly-sent-millions-to-nra-has-long-history-in-spain.

RT (2018a, June 27) OPCW granted right to assign guilt for chemical attacks after divisive UK proposal. *RT.com*. Available online at www.rt.com/news/431079-opcw-can-assign-guilt-chemical.

RT (2018b, July 31) Doomsday weapon': How could the West respond to Russia's nuclear underwater drone? *RT.com*. Available online at www.rt.com/op-ed/434759-drone-nuclear-poseidon-submarine/

RT (2018c, July 31) 'Skripal spoke to UK spies about the Russian mafia' – Seymour Hersh doubles down on Salisbury theory. *RT.com*. Available online at www.rt.com/uk/434755-skripal-salisbury-mafia-hersh.

RT (2019, January 21) First responder in Skripal poisoning turns out to be Britain's most senior military nurse. *RT.com*. Available online at www.rt.com/uk/449312-salisbury-first-resonder-identified.

Rutenberg, J. and Protess, B. (2018, July 21) Tabloid company, aiding Trump Campaign, may have crossed line into politics. *New York Times*. Available online at www.nytimes.com/2018/07/21/us/politics/trump-michael-cohen-american-media.html.

Sanger, D., Rutenberg, J. and E. Lipton (2018 July 15) Tracing Guccifer 2.0's many tentacles in the 2016 election. *New York Times*. Available online at www.nytimes.com/2018/07/15/us/politics/guccifer-russia-mueller.html.

Schecter, A. (2018, November 27) Mueller has emails from Stone pal Corsi about WikiLeaks Dem email dump. *NBCnews.com*. Available online at www.nbc news.com/politics/justice-department/mueller-has-emails-stone-pal-corsi-about-wikileaks-dem-email-n940611.

Schouten, F. (2018, July 13) Secret donors fund 40% of outside Congress ads. *Ventura County Star*, 6A.

Schwartz, J. (2018, November 1) The vulnerabilities of our voting machines. *Scientific American*. Available online at www.scientificamerican.com/article/the-vulnerabilities-of-our-voting-machines.

Schwirtz, M. (2017, September 21) German election mystery: Why no Russian meddling? *The New York Times*. Available online at www.nytimes.com/2017/09/21/world/europe/german-election-russia.html.

Schwirtz, M. and Barry, E. (2018, October 9) A spy story: Sergei Skripal was a little fish. He had a big enemy. *New York Times*. Available online at www.nytimes.com/2018/09/09/world/europe/sergei-skripal-russian-spy-poisoning.html.

Seetharaman, D. (2018, June 8) Facebook gave some companies special access to additional data about users' friends. *Wall Street Journal*. Available online at www.wsj.com/articles/facebook-gave-some-companies-access-to-additional-data-about-users-friends-1528490406.

Senate Select Committee on Intelligence (2018) *Russian targeting of election infrastructure during the 2016 election: Summary of initial findings and recommendations*. U.S. Senate, Washington D.C.

Serhan, Y. and Mahanta, S. (2018, March 22) What Russian scientists are saying about nerve agents. *The Atlantic*. Available online at www.theatlantic.com/international/archive/2018/03/what-we-know-about-Novichok/556148.

Shahtahmasebi, D. (2018, March 13) In Syria, media hypes enemy crimes and ignores ally's atrocities. *Anti-Media.com*. Available online at https://theantimedia. com/syria-media-hypes-eastern-ghouta-ignores-nato-turkey-afrin.

Shane, S. (2018, February 17). Russia isn't the only one meddling in elections. We do it, too. *New York Times*. Available online at www.nytimes.com/2018/02/17/sun day-review/russia-isnt-the-only-one-meddling-in-elections-we-do-it-too.html.

Shane, S. and Blinder, A. (2018, December 19) Secret experiment in Alabama senate race imitated Russian tactics. *New York Times*. Available online at www.nytimes. com/2018/12/19/us/alabama-senate-roy-jones-russia.html.

Shane, S. and Wakabayashi, D. (2018, April 4) 'The business of war': Google employees protest work for the Pentagon. *The New York Times*. Available online at www.nytimes.com/2018/04/04/technology/google-letter-ceo-pentagon-pro ject.html.

Shaw, M. (2016, December 16) Former British ambassador: Russia not the WikiLeaks source. *New American*. Available online at www.thenewamerican. com/tech/computers/item/24859-former-british-ambassador-russia-not-the-wiki leaks-source.

Sherman, M. (2018, June 11) Supreme Court allows Ohio, other state voter purges. *ABC News*. Available online at https://abcnews.go.com/Politics/wireStory/supreme-court-ohio-voter-purge-55805708.

Sheth, S. (2017, December 19) Former Director of National Intelligence James Clapper: Putin is handling Trump like a Russian 'asset.' *Business Insider*, available online at www.businessinsider.com/james-clapper-putin-trump-russia-asset-2017-12.

Shieber, J. (2018, March 16) Facebook suspends Cambridge Analytica, the data analysis firm that worked on the Trump campaign. *TechCrunch.com*. Available online at https://techcrunch.com/2018/03/16/facebook-suspends-cambridge-ana lytica-the-data-analysis-firm-that-worked-for-the-trump-campaign.

Sides, J., Tesler, M. and L. Vavreck (2018) *Identity crisis: The 2016 presidential campaign and the battle for the meaning of America*. Princeton, N.J.: Princeton University Press.

Simkin, J. (2014, August) *William Stephenson*. Spartacus Educational. Available online at http://spartacus-educational.com/2WWstephensonW.htm.

Sipher, J. (2017, September 6) A second look at the Steele dossier. Knowing what we know now. *Justsecurity.org*. Available online at www.justsecurity.org/44697/ steele-dossier-knowing.

Skiba, K. (2018, June 19) Two intelligence committees interested in Peter W. Smith, who sought Clinton emails from Russian hackers. *Chicago Tribune*. Available online at www.chicagotribune.com/news/local/politics/ct-met-peter-w-smith-congress-20171027-story.html.

Skwarkbox (2018, July 4) Newsnight admits what SKWAWKBOX said 2 days ago: Not just Russia can make Novichok. *Skwarkbox.org*. Available online at https:// skwawkbox.org/2018/04/07/newsnight-admits-what-skwawkbox-said-2-days-ago-not-just-russia-can-make-Novichok/

Slane, R. (2018) Thanks to the BBC propaganda show, the plausibility of the door handle theory just plummeted to freezing point. *The Blogmire.com*. Available online at www.theblogmire.com/thanks-to-the-bbc-propaganda-show-the-plausi bility-of-the-door-handle-theory-just-plummeted-to-freezing-point/

Smiley, L. (2017, November 1) The college kids doing what Twitter won't. *Wired. com*. Available online at www.wired.com/story/the-college-kids-doing-what-twitter-wont.

Solomon, J. (2018, June 25) How Comey intervened to kill WikiLeaks' immunity deal. *The Hill*. Available online at http://thehill.com/opinion/white-house/394036-How-Comey-intervened-to-kill-Wikileaks-immunity-deal.

SouthFront (2018) Russian Military Campaign in Syria 2015–2018. *SouthFront*. Available online at https://southfront.org/russian-military-campaign-in-syria-2015-2018/

Speakman, S. (2015, May 13) *Syrian Civil Defense: A framework for demobilization and reconstruction in post-conflict Syria*. Georgetown Security Studies Review. Available online at http://georgetownsecuritystudiesreview.org/2015/05/13/syrian-civil-defense-a-framework-for-demobilization-and-reconstruction-in-post-conflict-syria.

Special Counsel's Office (2018) *Related court documents*. Washington, DC: Department of Justice. Available online at www.justice.gov/sco.

Spring, T. (2018, May 3) Free speech advocates blast Amazon over threats against Signal. *Threatpost.com*. Available online at https://threatpost.com/free-speech-advocates-blast-amazon-over-threats-against-signal/131640/

Sputnik (2017, November 24) How author of 'Trump-Russia exposure' was stumped by Sputnik's questions. *Sputnik*. Available online at https://sputniknews.com/analysis/201711241059414892-us-trump-russia-harding.

Stahl, L. (2018, April 22) Aleksandr Kogan: The link between Cambridge Analytica and Facebook. *60 Minutes*. Available online at www.cbsnews.com/news/aleksandr-kogan-the-link-between-cambridge-analytica-and-facebook.

Statista (2018) Facebook's advertising revenue worldwide from 2009 to 2017 (in million U.S. dollars). *Statista*. Available online at www.statista.com/statistics/271258/facebooks-advertising-revenue-worldwide.

Stern, M. (2018, June 24) Why the Hollywood "resistance" must abandon Trump-friendly AMI. *The Daily Beast*. Available online at www.thedailybeast.com/why-resistance-hollywood-celebrities-must-abandon-trump-friendly-ami.

Stevens, R. (2019, January 7) UK Integrity Initiative heavily involved in Skripal affair. *World Socialist Web Site*. Available online at www.wsws.org/en/articles/2019/01/07/inte-j07.html.

Stockwell, J. (1987) America's Third World war. *Information clearing house*. Available online at www.informationclearinghouse.info/article4068.htm.

Strack, C. (2017, October) The evolution of the Islamic State's chemical weapons efforts. *CTC Sentinel at West Point*, 10(9). Available online at https://ctc.usma.edu/the-evolution-of-the-islamic-states-chemical-weapons-efforts/

Stuart, R. (2017) *Did the BBC lie? Media on Trial*. Available online at https://bbcpanoramasavingsyriaschildren.wordpress.com.

Sullivan, S. and Johnson, J. (2016, October 29) Yes, Donald Trump's crowds are big – but not quite as 'yuge' as he often claims. *The Washington Post*. Available online at www.washingtonpost.com.

Sultan, N. (2017, February 15) Pro-Israel interests upped contributions, lobbying in 2016. *OpenSecrets.org*. Available online at www.opensecrets.org/news/2017/02/pro-israel-interests-2016.

Sushi, B. (2018, April 14) A curious incident part IX. *The Saker*. Available online at https://thesaker.is/a-curious-incident-part-ix.

Syrmopoulos, J. (2018a, February 20) Kim Dotcom: DNC hack was leak from an "insider with a memory stick." *Truthinmedia.com*. Available online at http://truthinmedia.com/kim-dotcom-dnc-hack-insider-memory-stick/

Syrmopoulos, J. (2018b, April 18) American Journalist in Douma: Residents say chemical attack staged by 'terrorist rebels.' *Truthinmedia.com*. Available online at http://truthinmedia.com/american-journalist-in-douma-residents-say-chemical-attack-staged-by-terrorist-rebels/

Taub, A. and Fisher, M. (2018, February 18) Russian meddling was a drop in an ocean of American-made discord. *The New York Times*. Available online at www.nytimes.com/2018/02/18/world/europe/russia-us-election.html.

Taylor, A. (2018, February 18) The Russian journalist who helped uncover election interference is confounded by the Mueller indictments. *The Washington Post*. Available online at www.washingtonpost.com.

Taylor, L. (2014, October 14) Why so many House races (nearly all) are noncompetitive. *The Christian Science Monitor*. Available online at www.csmonitor.com/USA/Politics/Politics-Voices/2014/1014/Why-so-many-House-races-nearly-all-are-noncompetitive.

Tennison, S. (2018, February 6) Understanding Russia, Un-Demonizing Putin. *Consortiumnews.com*. Available online at https://consortiumnews.com/2018/02/06/understanding-russia-un-demonizing-putin.

The Saker (2018, November 2) "Russia Is preparing for war", senior Russian diplomat confirms. *Information Clearing House*. Available online at www.informationclearinghouse.info/50557.htm.

Thompson, M. (2015, May 29) How disbanding the Iraqi army fueled ISIS. *Time.com*. Available online at http://time.com/3900753/isis-iraq-syria-army-united-states-military.

Timberg, C. (2016, November 24) Russian propaganda effort helped spread 'fake news' during election, experts say. *Washington Post*. Available online at www.washingtonpost.com.

Timberg, C. and Harris, S. (2018 July 20) Russian operatives blasted 18,000 tweets ahead of a huge news day during the 2016 presidential campaign. Did they know what was coming? *SFGate*. Available online at www.sfgate.com/news/article/Russian-operatives-blasted-18-000-tweets-ahead-of-13092414.php.

Timmons, H. (2018, March 21) If Cambridge Analytica is so smart, why isn't Ted Cruz president? *Quartz*. Available online at https://qz.com/1234364/cambridge-analytica-worked-for-mercer-backed-ted-cruz-before-trump.

Tracy, A. (2017a, October 25) The dirty truth about the Steele dossier. *Vanity Fair*. Available online at www.vanityfair.com/news/2017/10/hillary-clinton-donald-trump-dossier.

Tracy, A. (2017b, November 14) What Does the WikiLeaks Bombshell Really Prove? Vanity Fair. Available online at www.vanityfair.com/news/2017/11/donald-trump-jr-wikileaks.

Tsuruoka, D. (2018, April 3) 'Star Wars' missile defense is back, but not how it should be. *AsiaTimes.com*. Available online at www.atimes.com/article/star-wars-missile-defense-back-not.

Tye, L. (2002) *The father of spin: Edward L. Bernays and the birth of public relations*. New York: Picador.

U.S. District Court of the District of Columbia (2018) Case 1:18-cr-00032-DLF: United States Of America V. Ira LLC A/K/A Mediasintez LLC A/K/A Glavset LLC A/K/A Mixinfo LLC A/K/A Azimut LLC A/K/A Novinfo LLC, Concord management and consulting LLC, concord catering, Yevgeniy Viktorovich, prigozhin, Mikhail Ivanovich Bystrov, Mikhail Leonidovich Burchik A/K/A Mikhail Abramov, Aleksandra Yuryevna Krylova, Anna Vladislavovna Bogacheva, Sergey Pavlovich Polozov, Maria Anatolyevna Bovda A/K/A Maria ANatolyevnabelyaeva, Robert Sergeyevich Bovda, Dzheykhun Nasimi Ogly Aslanov A/K/A Jayhoon Aslanov A/K/A Jay Aslanov, Vadim Vladimirovichpodkopaev, Gleb Igorevich Vasilchenko, Irina Viktorovna Kaverzina, and Vladimir Venkov. Defendants. Available online at www.justice.gov/sco.

UK Russian Embassy (The Embassy of the Russian Federation to the United Kingdom of Great Britain and Northern Ireland) (2018, June 29) *Embassy Press Officer's reply to a media question concerning statements of British Ambassador in Moscow Laurie Bristow for BBC Russian*. Press Release. Available online at www.rusemb.org.uk/fnapr/6574.

Unger, C. (2018) *House of Putin, House of Trump*. New York: Random House.

Urie, R. (2018, February 9) Why Russian meddling is a Trojan horse. *CounterPunch*. Available online at www.counterpunch.org/2018/02/09/why-russian-meddling-is-a-trojan-horse.

Van de Pijl, K. (2018) *Flight MH17, Ukraine and the new cold war: Prism of disaster*. Manchester: Manchester University Press.

Various (2017, September 1) A leak or a hack? A forum on the VIPS memo. *The Nation*. Available online at www.thenation.com/article/a-leak-or-a-hack-a-forum-on-the-vips-memo.

Vaughan-Nichols, S. (2018, March 18) How Cambridge Analytica used your Facebook data to help elect Trump. *ZDnet.com*. Available online at www.zdnet.com/article/how-cambridge-analytica-used-your-facebook-data-to-help-elect-trump.

Vos, E. (2018a, April 23) A conversation with Chris Blackburn on the contradictions surrounding Mifsud. *Disobedient Media*. Available online at https://disobedient media.com/2018/04/a-conversation-with-chris-blackburn-on-the-contradictions-surrounding-mifsud/

Vos, E. (2018b, May 11) All Russiagate roads lead to London as evidence emerges of Joseph Mifsud's links to UK intelligence. *Disobedient Media*. Available online at www.youtube.com/watch?v=yklmR5SxhVA.

Waldman, P. (2018, May 22) Get to know Elliott Broidy, the next major Trump scandal figure. *The Washington Post*. Available online at www.washingtonpost.com.

Walsh, J. (2018, September 18) Woodward: No evidence of Trump-Russia collusion. *The UNZ Review*. Available online at www.unz.com/article/woodward-no-evidence-of-trump-russia-collusion.

Washington Post (2018, April 24) Facebook reveals its censorship guidelines for the first time – 27 pages of them. *The Los Angeles Times*. Available online at www.latimes.com/business/technology/la-fi-tn-facebook-guidelines-20180424-story.html.

Webb, W. (2017a, July 31) James Le Mesurier: The former British mercenary who founded The White Helmets. *MintPressNews.com*. Available online at www.mint pressnews.com/james-le-mesurier-british-ex-military-mercenary-founded-white-helmets/230320.

Webb, W. (2017b, August 24) Your up-to-date guide to avoiding internet censorship & getting real watchdog journalism. *MintPressNews.com*. Available online at www.mintpressnews.com/date-guide-avoiding-internet-censorship/231253/

Webb, W. (2018a, April 21) US, fearing unfavorable OPCW results, blames Russia for "hacking" Dhouma evidence. *Mintpressnews.com*. Available online at www.mintpressnews.com/un-bows-to-western-pressure-blocks-opcw-team-from-investigating-douma-attacks/240860/

Webb, W. (2018b, June 21) Social media giants choking independent news site traffic to a trickle. *MintPressNews.com*. Available online at www.mintpressnews.com/social-media-giants-choking-independent-news-site-traffic-to-a-trickle/244471/

Webb, W. (2018c, August 2) "Inauthentic behavior:" Hysteria over newly revealed Facebook "Influence Campaign" doesn't fit the facts. *Social Mediocre*. Available online at https://socialmediocre.info/2018/08/02.

Webb, W. (2018d, October 30) The spin war: Collaboration of Bellingcat founder and ISIS Twitter account exposed in new report. *MintPressNews.com*. Available online at www.mintpressnews.com/collaboration-of-bellingcat-founder-and-isis-twitter-account-exposed-in-new-report/251185/

Weiss, C. (2018, December 24) Yet another murder that wasn't: The Perepilichny case and the anti-Russian campaign. *World Socialist Web Site*. Available online at www.wsws.org/en/articles/2018/12/24/pere-d24.html.

Wells, G. (2017, October 3) Russia-linked Facebook pages pushed divisions after election, including on Charlotsville. *Wall Street Journal*. Available online at www.wsj.com/articles/russia-linked-facebook-pages-pushed-divisive-views-through-august-1507051387.

West, D. (2018, June 28) More on the world of Christopher Steele and Russian agents, poisoned and un poisoned. *The American Spectator*. Available online at https://spectator.org/big-dots-do-they-connect.

Whitaker, B. (2018 June 27) Seymour Hersh on Syria: "There's no such thing as a chlorine bomb." Al-Bab.com. Available online at http://al-bab.com/blog/2018/06/seymour-hersh-syria-theres-no-such-thing-chlorine-bomb.

White, J. (2018, May 7) Facebook censors Arizona educators' rank-and-file committee group. *World Socialist Web Site*. Available online at www.wsws.org/en/articles/2018/05/07/cens-m07.html.

Whitney, M. (2016, December 16) So Putin didn't hack those emails after all. Counterpunch. Available online at www.counterpunch.org/2016/12/16/ah-so-put in-didnt-hack-those-emails-after-all.

Withers, P. (2018) No one looks that good after a chemical attack' Russia says Yulia Skripal interview staged. *Express*. Available online at www.express.co.uk/news/world/964587/russia-news-yulia-skripal-statement-interview-chemical-attack-kremlin.

Wittner, L. (2018, June 18) Trump's getting us ready to fight a nuclear war. *History newsnetwork.org*. https://historynewsnetwork.org/article/169323.

Woodward, B. (2018) *Fear: Trump in the Whitehouse*. New York: Simon and Schuster.

Zenco, M. (2016, July 5) Do not believe the U.S. government's official numbers on drone strike civilian casualties. *Foreignpolicy.com*. Available online at http://foreignpolicy.com/2016/07/05/do-not-believe-the-u-s-governments-official-numbers-on-drone-strike-civilian-casualties.

Zero, M. (2018, October 8) The CIA finger in Brasil's elections. *Information Clearing House*. Available online at www.informationclearinghouse.info/50395.htm.

Zetter, K. (2018a, February 21) The myth of the hacker-proof voting machine. *New York Times*. Available online at www.nytimes.com/2018/02/21/magazine/the-myth-of-the-hacker-proof-voting-machine.html.

Zetter, K. (2018b, July 17) Top voting machine vendor admits it installed remote-access software on systems sold to states. *Motherboad.vice.com*. Available online at https://motherboard.vice.com/en_us/article/mb4ezy/top-voting-machine-vendor-admits-it-installed-remote-access-software-on-systems-sold-to-states.

Zhen, L. (2018, August 6) China's hypersonic aircraft, Starry Sky-2, could be used to carry nuclear missiles at six times the speed of sound. *South China Morning Post*. Available online at www.scmp.com/news/china/diplomacy-defence/article/2158524/chinas-hypersonic-aircraft-starry-sky-2-could-be-used.

Zurcher, A. (2016, November 6) Hillary Clinton emails – what's it all about? *BBC*. Available online at www.bbc.com/news/world-us-canada-31806907.

Index

For Product Safety Concerns and Information please contact our EU
representative GPSR@taylorandfrancis.com
Taylor & Francis Verlag GmbH, Kaufingerstraße 24, 80331 München, Germany